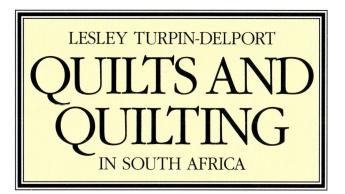

LESLEY TURPIN-DELPORT
QUILTS AND QUILTING
IN SOUTH AFRICA

Dedication
To the quilter who works
with her hands in delight.
(ADAPTED FROM PROVERBS 31)

LESLEY TURPIN-DELPORT
QUILTS AND QUILTING
IN SOUTH AFRICA

STRUIK TIMMINS

HALF TITLE
Quilt artist: **Jessica van Niekerk**
A detail showing the traditional feathered star design, which has been hand pieced and hand quilted. Notice the echo quilting in the floral patches.

TITLE PAGE
Quilt artist: **Jackie Crook**
Details of *Islands in the stream* showing a machine strip-pieced background in raw silk, chintz and corded cotton balanced by the machine-appliquéd island.

PAGES 8 & 9
Quilt artist: **Village Quilters, Kloof**
A simple patchwork block comes together in a group effort. Each midline block is bordered with beautiful embroidery stitches which add to the Victorian charm of this quilt. Once all the blocks were machine pieced together, the complementary squares formed by the piecing were hand quilted.

PAGES 24 & 25
Quilt artist: **Lee Hackman**
This machine-pieced, hand-quilted work shows all the elements of basic design: line, form and composition.

PAGES 32 & 33
Quilt artist: **Roy Starke**
This detail shows an asymetrical design and areas of strip piecing in a machine-pieced, hand-quilted and painted quilt with beads, embroidery and appliqué.

PAGES 66 & 67
Quilt artist: **Jolena van Rooyen**
Detail of a superb quilt by this talented artist. A combination of appliqué, patchwork and quilting was used in this prize-winning quilt.

PAGES 90 & 91
Quilt artist: **Marion Berkowitz**
Exciting composite stitches and vibrant colours mingle to make a marvellous composition.

PUBLISHER'S ACKNOWLEDGEMENTS
The Publisher wishes to thank Rosalie Dace for graciously permitting the use of the quilt depicted on the front cover and Margee Gough for those on the back cover.

AUTHOR'S ACKNOWLEDGEMENTS
My special thanks to all the quilters who have contributed to this book, to photographers Charles Corbett, Kurt Lossgott, Ronnie Rogoff and Kevin Taylor and to my family and friends who have shown so much patience and understanding during the production of this book.

Quilt artist: **Isabel Scott**

Quilt artist: **Roy Starke**

Struik Timmins Publishers (Pty) Ltd
(a member of The Struik Group (Pty) Ltd)
Struik House
80 McKenzie Street
Cape Town 8001

Reg. No.: 54/00965/07

First published 1991

Copyright © text, illustrations and photographs Lesley Turpin-Delport 1991

All rights reserved. No part of this publication may be reproduced, stored in a retrieval system, or transmitted, in any form or by any means, electronic, mechanical, photocopying or otherwise, without the prior written permission of the copyright owner.

Editors: Aletta van der Westhuizen and Linda de Villiers
Designer: Janice Evans
Cover design: Janice Evans
Cover photographs: (Front cover) *Fair Lady* magazine; (Back cover) Ronnie Rogoff
Layout artist: Lellyn Creamer
Illustrations: Jacques Le Roux (pages 10-105) and Clarence Clarke (pages 106-158)

Typesetting by Diatype Setting cc, Cape Town
Reproduction by Unifoto Ltd, Cape Town
Printed and bound by Leefung-Asco Printers Ltd, Hong Kong

ISBN 0 86978 517 3

CONTENTS

Introduction 7
Quilting Basics 9
Quilting Options 25
Piecing and Quilting 33
Appliqué and Quilting 67
Embroidery and Quilting 91
Templates 106
Quilters Shopping Guide 159
Further Reading 159
Quilting Teachers 159
Index 160

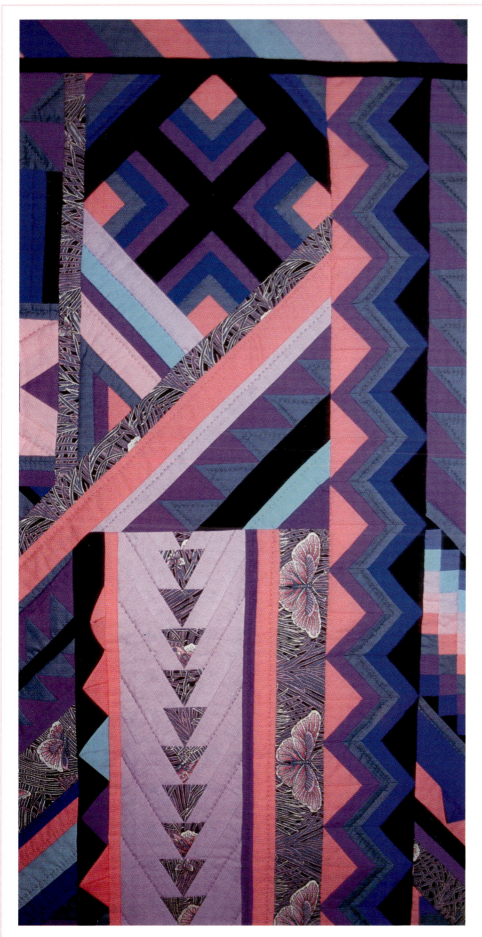

Quilt artist: **Margaret Le Roux**

INTRODUCTION

Fibre is a fundamental and complex expression of civilization, both the by-product of a need for covering and an inexhaustible medium through which creative impulses can be channelled. Textiles have always been popular with folk craftsmen but now you can see an awareness of creativity in the use of fabric in the context of fine art. These new fabric artworks are exemplified in amazing quilts, which can range from miniature quilts and fabric collages to bed quilts and mighty wall hangings.

In this book I have tried to combine a basic 'how to' with visual stimuli to inspire you to experiment and to 'paint with fabric' so that you can reach your full potential as a quilt designer. As a quilt-maker, you must enjoy the process of making a quilt and sharing its beauty with others. Visit quilt exhibitions to see and appreciate other quilts. Whether you feel more comfortable with nostalgic, traditional designs or find excitement in the new lines and colours of modern quilts, this book will provide wonderfully stimulating ideas that you can translate into totally original quilts merely by changes in your choice of fabric, colour and thread. For instance, you may wish to take a traditional block and to transform it into a haphazard design like the Afro-American quilts depicted on pages 58 and 59, or adapt a basic log cabin to create an original design such as those featured on pages 42 and 43.

If this is your first attempt at quilt-making, I have included numerous step-by-step instructions which simplify a host of techniques ranging from quilting and embroidery to piecing and appliqué. You can begin with the more simple techniques and as your ability increases, you can graduate to combining two or more techniques to create quilts of increasing complexity. With knowledge and imagination, there is no limit to what you can achieve.

I am immensely proud to be able to include not only my own work and that of my students, but also that of the many quilt-makers from all over South Africa. These highly talented artists have generously shared their expertise and graciously allowed their work to be included in this book.

I hope that you will find this book inspirational and that you will create a quilt or many quilts that will be treasured forever.

Lesley Turpin-Delport

OPPOSITE
Artist: Denise Schlesinger (Edelmuth Studio)
Cords of different thicknesses have been used to create the bark while coils pulled from the cord create foliage in this exquisite appliqué entitled *Trees*.

CHAPTER ONE
QUILTING BASICS

BASIC EQUIPMENT

TOOLS FOR MARKING

There are a number of different marking tools to choose from. The best choice is the tool that gives a clear, visible line that shows while you work but not once the quilt is complete.

Pencils

Pencils work well and generally show up on light-coloured fabrics. Although different types are available, it is best to use a soft pencil (4B or 6B) as the graphite does not penetrate the fibres and thus washes out successfully. A hard pencil (H or 2H) makes a light, fine line which doesn't wash out as easily as the softer pencil. Mark the design with a broken line or dots. Make sure your pencil is very sharp.

Dressmaker's pencils *(Chalk pencils)*

These pencils come in blue, pink and white and show up on all coloured fabrics. They need regular sharpening however and often fade as you work. You might have to re-mark the quilting line a couple of times. There are also silver-coloured pencils on the market that are fairly successful.

Water-soluble pens

These are usually turquoise-coloured 'felt-tipped' pens which are ideal for marking light- and medium-coloured fabrics. Unwanted lines can be dabbed out with cold water and once the quilt is complete, the entire quilt can be dipped into or washed in cold water to remove all the marks. However, these pens do have a few disadvantages: they cannot be used on fabrics that need to be dry cleaned; the bright blue colour can be distracting when one is working on a pastel quilt; and in humid weather the colour fades rapidly. Some quilters believe that the use of commercial pens may even damage the fibre of quilts made for posterity.

NOTE: *There are a number of dark, fine-line marking pens which are supposed to wash out, but do test these pens on a scrap of your quilt fabric as they are not always water soluble.*

Soap

The thin slivers of soap that most of us throw away mark dark fabrics very well and obviously wash out with ease.

Dressmaker's carbon and a tracing wheel

These can also be used to mark the quilting design on the fabric. Sandwich the carbon paper between the design and the fabric and, using the wheel, trace over the lines to transfer the design onto the fabric.

Rulers

Excellent quilting rulers marked with geometric measurements are available from specialist quilting stores and make quilt designing much easier.

Narrow masking tape

This can also be used for marking straight lines.

Stencils

Traditional quilt stencils are available for fancy curved designs such as cables, feathers and wreaths.

Templates

Paper or cardboard templates (see page 34) are easy to make. These consist of a basic outline which can be filled with additional details, and can be used repeatedly over the surface of the quilt.

THIMBLES

Thimbles are essential for hand quilting. Use a thimble which is a comfortable fit on the middle finger of your sewing hand.

Thimbles come in all shapes and sizes in metal, leather and plastic and most people have their own preference. Just remember that the thimble is needed to guide the needle through all the layers, allowing several stitches to be taken at once.

Some quilters use a thimble on the hand that works the underside of the quilt and others even use a metal teaspoon. I like to be able to feel and anticipate the needle on the underside to make small, even stitches.

NEEDLES

Short, fine needles are best for hand quilting. Use the needle called a 'between' (No. 10).

THREAD

Commercial quilting threads are now available in all colours but if you can't find any, use a pure cotton thread (No. 30) and run it through beeswax to prevent it tangling.

WADDING *(Batting)*

This is the key ingredient that gives the quilt the plumpness and indentations that create visual and actual texture. Today we have washable polyester wadding in many different thicknesses. The thicker the wadding, the more difficult it is to make tiny stitches. Use the thick wadding only for quilts that are not too large and will not be washed. The ideal wadding is a thin, bonded polyester in which the fibres are bonded together with a warp and a weft. Bundles of polyester wadding are used for trapunto quilting (page 26), where small cavities are stuffed to give a high-relief effect.

> **TO JOIN PIECES OF WADDING**
> *If wadding has to be joined there are a couple of different methods depending on the type of wadding being used:*
> ❑ *If the wadding is very thin and can be joined before the quilt is assembled, overlap the two edges and machine zigzag the join.*
>
>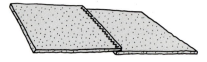
>
> ❑ *If the wadding is fairly thick, splice the two pieces together by halving the thickness on each piece and overlapping the edges so that there is no extra thickness.*
>
>
>
> ❑ *If the blocks are already joined with the 'quilt-as-you-go' method, butt the two edges of the wadding together and join them with herringbone stitch.*
>
>

FABRICS

Natural fibres such as cottons, lawns, silks and wools are most suitable for *hand quilting*. Wash your fabric to remove any dressing as this will make the fabric easier to work with. Choose fabrics that are not too closely woven so that the needle can pierce the fabric easily. The quilting stitch shows up more clearly on plain fabrics than on prints, but often the printed fabric will suggest a quilting design that will complement the whole quilt. The ideal fabric for an antique look or neutral background is seedcloth which is an unbleached 100% pure cotton.

Synthetic fabrics and mixed weights are more suitable for *machine quilting* since they often present problems for hand sewing.

HOOPS AND FRAMES

A hoop or frame is used to hold the layers of the quilt firmly together and to keep the surface evenly stretched for hand quilting.

Hoops

These are handy for quilters who like to take their quilting blocks with them and work wherever they can. The hoop holds the work taut between an inner ring and an outer ring which can be adjusted by tightening or loosening a screw. The sizes vary from 30 cm (12 in) to 61 cm (24 in). The hoop can also be supported by a lap stand or a pedestal stand which leaves both hands free.

Frames

Antique quilts were almost always worked on a frame. The ladies would get together for a 'quilting bee' and spend many hours quilting on one frame. The frame can be set up and left for the quilter to return at his or her leisure. The fabric is handled less and can be quilted right up to the edge. There are a number of different frames on the market: I prefer a simple design made up of two runners and two stretchers which can be supported on trestles or a table top.

Quilt artist: **Lesley Turpin-Delport**
Detail of a Baltimore quilt in progress. Turkey work (page 95) has been used to create the bee's body.

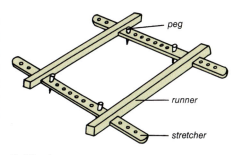

Quilting frame

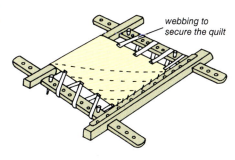

Quilting frame with the quilt already assembled

Quilting hoop supported by a pedestal

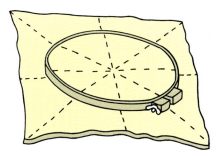

Quilting hoop

PATTERN AND COLOUR

The success of a quilt hinges largely on the choice of colour and fabric.

COLOUR
Colour can make or break a design. The colour wheel is a good guide, although colour choice is personal.

Complementary colours (opposite colours on the wheel such as red-green, yellow-purple, orange-blue) give a visual vibration.

Primary colours (red, yellow and blue) are dominant because they are the purest colours. Juxtaposed colours (those colours next to each other on the colour wheel such as blue, green and violet) blend together softly.

Tones (colours mixed with grey) and *tints* (colours mixed with white) give subtle nuances because of their subdued nature.

Neutral colours (black, white and grey) work well with almost any colour.

The illustrations provided here should help towards a better understanding of colour and fabric choice.

The colour wheel can also be divided into *warm* and *cool* colours (see illustration opposite). As warm colours seem to come towards you and cool colours seem to recede, a feeling of depth can be achieved by combining both warm and cool colours.

PATTERN
Solid colours and prints are equally successful in appliquéd or pieced quilts. Some designers combine both while other quilters, such as the Amish, prefer solids (plain fabric). The plain, limited palette of the Amish results in strong, powerful quilts.

Fabric colours can range from light to medium to dark, while the scale of the prints can vary from small to medium to large. Some prints have overall motifs while others are isolated.

Background fabric, as used in Amish quilts, can be plain, either in a dark or light colour. A small print used for the background, however, can give the illusion of texture, a dark background will be dramatic, while a pale background lends itself to the linear rhythms of a

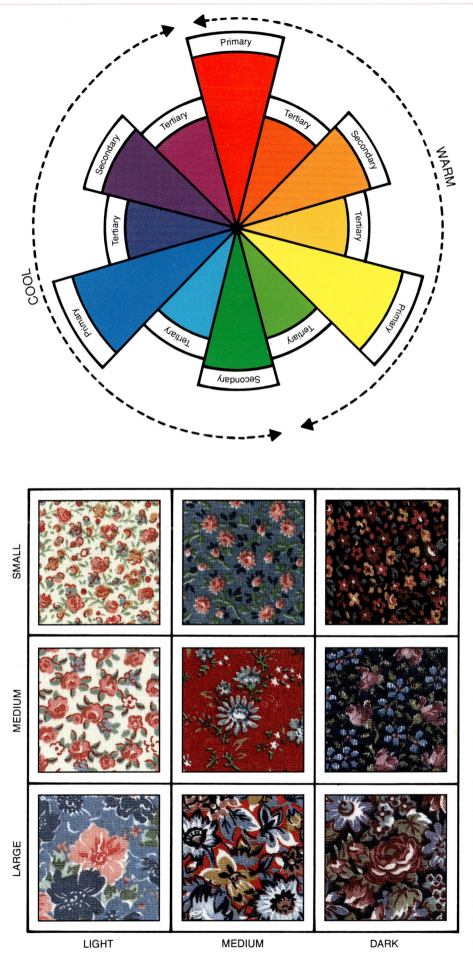

quilted line. Printed border designs can be very useful as sashing or for the outer borders on a quilt.

Be careful with large geometric prints; fabric designs with too much white in the background; one-way designs or busy prints. It is best to choose fabrics with designs that will not interfere in any way with the piecing, appliquéing or quilting process.

Quilt artist: **Lydia Fouché**
Detail of a stunning stained-glass quilt. The graded colours follow the spectrum of the colour wheel, with unexpected highlights creating a zigzag rhythm.

COLOURING YOUR OWN FABRIC

If the available fabric is not suitable for your design, the fabric can always be dyed, batik dyed, hand- or spray-painted, or marbled to create a more personal effect. Remember to wash the fabric before proceeding (see *Fabrics* page 10).

Tea is an outstanding dye and changes a bright white into a pinky ecru. Pour boiling water over the tea bags. Once all the tannin has soaked out of the bags, remove them from the solution and submerge the fabric in the tea solution. Remove the fabric after 10 minutes and place it in a boiling solution of vinegar and water. Use 2 litres (½ gallon) of water to 125 ml (½ cup) of vinegar.

After the solution has cooled, remove the fabric and rinse it thoroughly in cold water.

Paint There are a number of different paint techniques that you can use. For instance, some of my students use an aerosol spray paint (or an airbrush) to give background illusions to the fabric; some use silk paint on seedcloth (unbleached 100% pure cotton fabric) and make prints from foliage or cut-outs from carrots or potatoes; while others use stencil paint on gauze bandage to add to the sensitivity of a background in a freestyle landscape.

Marbling or dyeing your fabric can be the perfect solution if 'bought' fabrics are not suitable.

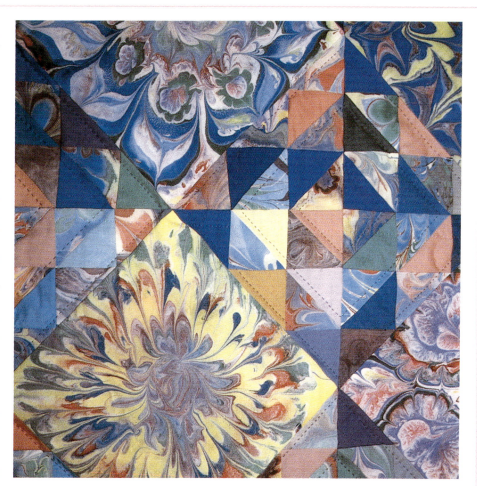

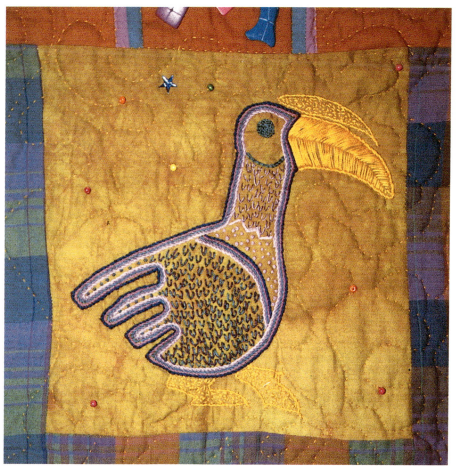

OPPOSITE
Quilt artist: **Leonie Segal**
Paint, hessian, organza and tulle have been worked into an unusual composition with embroidery details in this mixed media *Landscape*.

ABOVE RIGHT
Quilt artist: **Jackie Fletcher**
A detail from a quilt showing marbled fabric. The outline quilting reinforces the patchwork design and stabilizes the movement created by the fluid lines of the paint.

RIGHT
Quilt artist: **Sue Funston**
This detail shows tie-dyed and batiked fabric which the artist has embellished with embroidery, quilting and beads.

THE QUILT LAYOUT
Planning the layout of the quilt is probably one of the key ingredients to a successful quilt. The basic layout is the way in which the components are put together to create an overall effect. The following sketches should give you some ideas for layouts:

Strip layout or standard bars

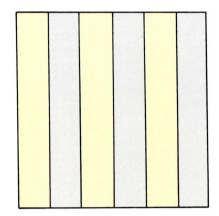

Straight

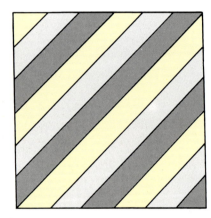

Diagonal

Block layout

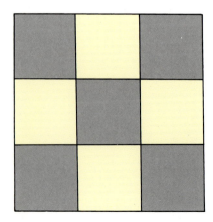

Straight

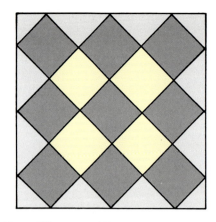

Diagonal (Square on point)

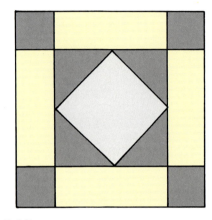

Medallion

Random

A number of layouts can be combined very successfully for a quilt top. For instance a medallion centre can be framed by a diamond layout and finished with a border of square blocks.

The size of a quilt can be increased by elongating or widening the blocks.

Sashing
This is an interesting way of adding extra dimensions to the quilt layout. The sashing provides a break in the design and the opportunity for additional quilting patterns.

Sashing can be used between the blocks of a quilt to bring the quilt up to the required size. It can be in neutral fabric, which lends itself to exotic quilting patterns; in a patterned fabric which complements the blocks; or even in wide, border lace. The arrangement of blocks to sashing can be on the horizontal or on the vertical plane as shown. The width of the sashing will depend on the size of the blocks and the basic quilt design. (Obviously all the parts of the quilt must be in pleasing proportions.)

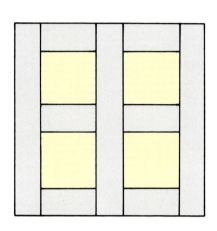

Vertical sashing

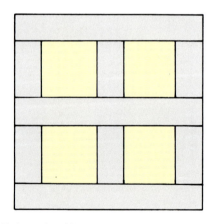

Horizontal sashing

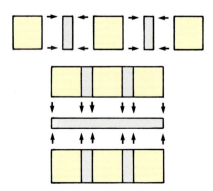

Attach the short pieces of sashing, then the long pieces.

16

MATTRESS MEASUREMENTS
When planning the layout of a quilt, bear in mind that finished blocks usually cover only the top of the mattress. As a border (see below) is added for the overhang, its width will depend on how much overhang you require on each side. The following mattress measurements will assist you when planning a quilt:

Cot	70 x 127 cm (27½ x 50 in)
Single bed	91 x 190 cm (36 x 75 in)
Double bed	137 x 190 cm (54 x 75 in)
Queen size	150 x 203 cm (60 x 80 in)
King size	180 x 203 cm (71 x 80 in)

Borders

Although traditional quilts usually have borders, not every quilt will require one. Study the basic design of your quilt and assess whether it needs a border. You may wish to add a border to make the quilt larger; to balance a complex appliquéd or pieced design with a plain colour; to frame the quilt top; or to allow a change in rhythm, for example from a central design to another idea which will suit the vertical fall on the mattress side.

You must plan your border at the beginning of the designing stage, but as the quilt progresses certain changes can be made if necessary.

Instructions on how to assemble the borders are given on page 60. The following tips will give you some ideas for border design:

❏ If the design runs off into space it will need a border
❏ A repeat element, such as a triangle for example, will help to stabilize a busy quilt design
❏ Use some elements which appear in the central theme for the border – colour, shapes, fabric or lines
❏ Use the shapes in the border to create movement

The border must complement the main design; it must not overwhelm the centre or be insignificant. As it should define the quilt, medium- or dark-coloured fabrics are usually most successful.

BELOW LEFT
Quilt artist: **Margee Gough**
The sashing fabric in deep red and jade green tones with all the enamel badges. The sashing is made up of short horizontals and long verticals and the outline quilting helps one to focus on each quilting badge in turn.

BELOW
Quilt artist: **Riet van Aiden**
Although each block is different, this quilt works as the mustard-coloured sashing encloses the different appliqué and patchwork designs.

Creating your own design

Nature offers a marvellous source of inspiration – floral shapes, landscapes (earth, sea and sky) and creatures. The choice is limitless.

Great works of art, children's drawings, wrapping paper and greetings cards can all provide inspiration for appliqué and piecing. As in any design, basic art principles governing colour, line, space, shape, repetition and texture will apply.

LEFT

Quilt artist: **Celia de Villiers**
Awarded first prize in the ethnic section of a quilt festival, this batik-dyed wall-hanging of raw shantung is enveloped by a strip-pieced curtain of African print, snakeskin, feather leather and lamé fabric. The 'pattern of bones' has been hand pieced with the English inlay method and the headdress beaded with authentic sangoma-wig beads. The verse below was written especially for *Sangoma*.

'She stares across time in the very heart of life itself. For she is the symbol of motherhood, safety, trust and comfort. The mother of men, who understands many hidden things. In her protective hand the sacred stone Haematite: giver of life, power and healing. Around her neck the pod; that secret womb filled with the seeds of living forces. What does she read from the pattern of bones? She is exceedingly wise, this medicine woman, for she has lived in both worlds. Notice the rich fabrics around her symbol of the glitzy city. Nearby, her own African fabrics. Africa! Where man arose from a bed of reeds to carry on the mysteries. But where is the answer? . . . She knows . . . oh yes . . . But she keeps her silence'

FIONA OGILVY

ABOVE OPPOSITE

Quilt artist: **Julia Clephane**
Detail of a quilt *Autumn in London* showing how an *idea* is seen through in colour suggestions and quilting rhythms. Notice how the outline, diagonal and free-flowing quilting helps to balance the strong diagonals created by the fabric.

OPPOSITE

Quilt artist: **Julia Clephane**
In *White Nights* there is a brilliant balance of light against dark. Notice the quilting in silver metallic thread.

OPPOSITE
Quilt artist: **Valerie Hearder**
This masterful composition of abstract shapes was inspired by the African beaded apron. The play of light and shade is enhanced by the choice of colour, fabric and texture.

RIGHT
Quilt artist: **Jutta Faulds**
This commemorative vestment was designed after devastating floods ravaged Natal, South Africa. Elements of appliqué, embroidery, patchwork and 'found' objects have been used to construct five panels which tell the tale from the destruction, the flotsum, burying the dead, the fund-raising and finally the Resurrection after the floods. Here are three of the panels, depicting the Resurrection (right), burying the dead (below left) and the destruction (below right).

Quilt artist: **Lina Lombard**
This design is based on five-point, six-point and eight-point stars. Note the superbly sensitive use of subdued colour, the strip-pieced inner border and large outer border. Circular quilting rhythms add movement to the negative spaces of this prize-winning quilt.

Quilt artist: **Janet Roche**
Composite embroidery stitches and trapunto quilting make up this panel showing the signing of a quilt.

COMPETITIONS

COMPETITION POINTS

For quilters interested in entering competitions, it is useful to know that the judges assess each quilt for workmanship and design and award points on the following criteria on a scale of excellent, very good, good and moderate.

Workmanship
Accuracy of construction
Quilting technique
Edge or binding
Backing
General standard

Design
Visual impact
Overall design
Use of colour
Creativity
Quilting design

COMMENTS AND EXHIBITION REQUIREMENTS

A final assessment of the above points can put your quilt into a prizewinning category.

Do notice how important the finish of your quilt is; the backing and the edge or binding form an integral part of the overall appearance of the quilt.

The quilt should have a name, date and signature on it. You can embroider this information onto the front of the quilt in fine back stitch, provided it does not detract from the quilt design. Otherwise, embroider the details on the back.

For exhibition purposes, should there be any information of interest, or group workers' names, write the details in indelible ink (or embroider them) on a separate piece of fabric and hand hem it to the back of the quilt.

Your quilt will need a sleeve sewn onto the back of the top edge so that the quilt can be hung at a quilt show. The 'sleeve' is also ideal if the quilt is intended as a wall decoration and not for a bed.

Making a sleeve

1. Cut a strip of calico approximately 18 cm (7 in) wide and the length of the top of the quilt.

2. Turn the short ends under and machine stitch. Fold the strip in half lengthwise, right sides together, and stitch a 6 mm (¼ in) seam along the long raw edge.

3. Turn the tube right side out and press the seam lightly.

4. Using a strong thread, whip stitch the upper and lower edges of the tube to the top of the back of the quilt, just below the binding.

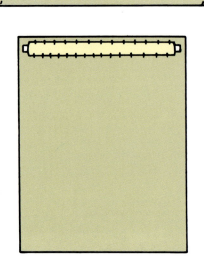

ABOVE
Quilt artist: **Nicola Delport**
Painted spots and candlewick knots vie for dominance on the prickly pear plant. The octopus suckers are metal washers covered with buttonhole stitch in candlewick cotton No. 8.

TOP
Sea anemones, photographed by G M Branch, can act as inspiration and be interpreted in mixed media as shown above.

ABOVE RIGHT
Quilt artist: **Nicola Delport**
A tactile quilt in every sense of the word. Spatial movement is enhanced by underpainting with stencil paints.

RIGHT
Quilt artist: **Margaret Le Roux**
This design was inspired by a piece of wrapping paper. Details show the exciting choices of fabric for the border design and precise piecing of the headgear.

CHAPTER TWO
QUILTING OPTIONS

Quilting is both functional and decorative in that it provides warmth and design interest. The quilting stitches hold the wadding in place and keep it from bunching. Stitches either follow the outline of the shapes in the design or they create decorative patterns on the background. Quilting can be done by hand with a small running stitch or by machine.

PREPARATION

Before you can begin quilting, it is necessary first to transfer the design onto the fabric and then to tack together the three layers required for quilting.

MARKING

It is easiest to mark the designs directly onto the top fabric before tacking the three layers together.

Divide the surface of the fabric into smaller areas by ironing or tacking to create a grid which will help you to centre the quilting design.

Choose your marking tool (page 10) and trace the designs onto the right side of the fabric.

TACKING

The three layers required for quilting are the essence of the quilt, while the quilting stitches that travel through and secure the layers define the design of the quilt.

The 'textile sandwich' is made up of the lining, the wadding and the ground (top) fabric. Before you begin quilting, tack the three layers together: first the lining, wrong side up, then the wadding, and finally the ground fabric, right side up. Tack outwards from the centre towards each of the corners, making sure that the radiating tacking lanes are not more than two to three finger widths apart. End the tacking at the outer edge with a quilting knot or a back stitch (see page 28).

An unorthodox method of tacking is to pin the layers together with brass safety pins available from specialist quilting stores.

Insert the prepared quilt into a hoop or frame and you are ready to begin the quilting process.

QUILTING TECHNIQUES

There are a number of different quilting techniques, ranging from high relief (trapunto) to merely the suggestion of quilted rhythms (such as echo quilting).

As there are so many techniques to choose from, it is important to select one that will enhance your design. Plan your quilting designs very carefully. The quilting must form an integral part of the quilt, yet it must be able to stand on its own as a total design on the reverse of the quilt.

Quilting creates the texture of the quilt and wonderful effects can be achieved by cleverly balancing densely quilted areas against the more open designs.

All the techniques discussed below (except trapunto and corded quilting) use the 'textile sandwich' (see page 26) as their base and the finished effect is low relief.

QUILTING IN THE DITCH

This technique is often used with patchwork piecing. Make the stitches on the seam line, between the fabrics. The stitches do not show and the area surrounded by the quilting stitches is defined.

ECHO (Contour) QUILTING

This is a simple method of quilting which echoes the outlines of the basic design until the background space is filled. Begin at the outer edge of the motif and move outwards at regular intervals of about 6 mm (¼ in) or at increasing intervals. Very close parallel lines of tiny stitches give a ripple effect, creating an overall texture.

To create echo quilting by machine, position the foot next to the motif and straight stitch around the design using the foot as your space guide. Continue quilting until the entire background is patterned.

OUTLINE QUILTING

This is the method most commonly used on pieced quilts. Follow the outline of the motif approximately 6 mm (¼ in) inside or outside the basic shape. This quilting technique accentuates the motif and gives extra body to the shape.

Usually only a single line of quilting stitches is used, as opposed to echo (contour) quilting which consists of many parallel lines of quilting.

FILLER QUILTING

Here straight or curved lines are used to fill large, empty areas or to create elaborate designs. Diagonal or lattice quilting (cross-hatching) is often used to achieve an overall effect.

QUILTING IN PATTERNS

Motifs can be made in many different shapes, such as flowers, shells or scallops, and can be used singly or as repeat designs. This type of quilting is done in large negative spaces for added interest or on borders.

TRAPUNTO AND CORDED QUILTING

Trapunto and corded quilting are both high-relief techniques which use a ground fabric and a lining (muslin) as their basic ingredients. After the design has been padded (see below), the background can be quilted using the 'textile sandwich' and the relevant quilting technique.

Trapunto

This is also called high-relief quilting and is an attractive form of quilting where selected areas of the design are padded to give a raised effect.

1. Cut a piece of background fabric and a corresponding piece of muslin.

2. Transfer the quilting design onto the fabric using a dressmaker's pencil or an erasable marking pen.

3. Tack the ground fabric and muslin together. Secure the fabrics in a quilting hoop and stitch along the design lines using either running stitch or a decorative stitch, keeping your stitches small and even.

4. Make a small slit in the muslin in the centre of each shape to be padded, or preferably push the

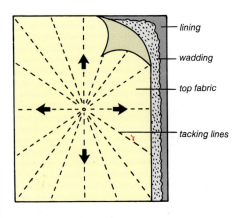

Textile Sandwich

weave aside, and insert small pieces of polyester wadding through the slit with a toothpick or crochet hook until the shape is evenly padded on the right side. Some areas can be padded more than others to create a more three-dimensional effect.

5. *Sew up the slits with tiny whip stitches or push the weave together with a toothpick.*

Trapunto is complemented by background quilting such as echo quilting or by embroidering French knots or colonial knots at regular intervals.

Trapunto and embroidery can also be combined successfully. Instead of running stitches, trapunto outlines can be embroidered with chain stitch, French knots or colonial knots (as seen in candlewicking, page 102).

Corded quilting
Sometimes also called Italian quilting, this type of quilting gives an attractive raised effect and is particularly suitable for linear patterns.

1. *Transfer the designs onto the fabric, then join the top fabric and the backing fabric (muslin) together with diagonal, horizontal or vertical lines of tacking.*

2. *Machine straight stitch, or stitch by hand using back stitch or a running stitch, along the parallel lines of the designs.*

3. *Working from the back and using a blunt bodkin or tapestry needle threaded with quilting wool or cord, pad the lines of the design. Insert the threaded needle between the two layers of fabric, inside the two parallel lines.*

4. *Tie off the cord by making a small back stitch into the backing fabric, or if the cord exits close to the beginning, knot the two ends of the cord together. Do not pull the cord too tight – leave a little slack in case of shrinkage when the item is washed.*

TOP RIGHT
Quilt artist: **Suzette Ehlers**
This is a beautiful example of abstract, freestyle quilting, which creates new rhythms within the confines of the piecing.

RIGHT
Quilt artist: **Mary Morris**
Each section of the basic block has been quilted in a design that enhances that particular shape. The quilting designs are clearly visible on the reverse side of the quilt.

FAR RIGHT ABOVE
Quilt artist: **Lesley Lewis**
One of a series of panels for a wall quilt. The echo quilting creates rhythm and texture in the design.

FAR RIGHT BELOW
Quilt artist: **Janet Roche**
A fine example of floral embroidery, trapunto and echo quilting.

HOW TO BEGIN THE QUILTING STITCH
Cut a length of quilting thread, not longer than 50 cm (about 20 in), thread it into your No 10 'between' needle and make a knot in the thread.

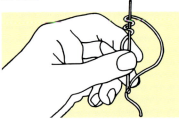

Insert the needle into the top fabric and pull the thread so that the knot goes through the fabric, anchoring itself in the wadding to nestle just beneath the top fabric. Make a back stitch before proceeding with the quilting stitch.

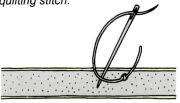

HOW TO END THE QUILTING STITCH
Before making your last stitch, make a knot in the quilting thread near the fabric, then make a back stitch and pull the thread through so that the knot penetrates the wadding. Lose the end of the thread in the wadding and trim off.

An alternative method is the **half back stitch**. Make a small back stitch into the previous stitch splitting the thread of the stitch. Lose the end of the thread in the wadding.

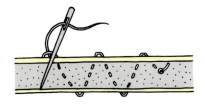

HAND QUILTING

Hand quilting is worked with small, evenly spaced running stitches. It sounds relatively simple but does take practice to perfect. The thread stitches should be as small as possible and the fabric spaces should be even, but not necessarily as small as the quilting stitches. The thickness of the wadding will dictate the size of the stitch. The quilting stitch should be as good on the underside of the quilt as on the top. There are three different methods of making the quilting stitch – *stab stitching*, *single stitching* and *rocker quilting*. The choice is personal and all are acceptable if they are well executed.

STAB STITCH

Working with a thimble on the middle finger of your sewing hand, push the needle down through the three layers, and then up, in two separate movements. Keep your other hand under the quilt to pull the needle through. This method is slow and not very accurate but is handy if the fabric is very thick (for example with appliqué), if the seam is multi-layered or if the wadding is too thick for rocker quilting.

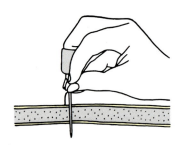

SINGLE STITCHING

Single stitching is more accurate than stab stitching. Working from the top, push the needle in and out of the fabric in a single movement. Extend the thumb on your sewing hand to press the fabric down just ahead of the point of the needle as it exits on top.

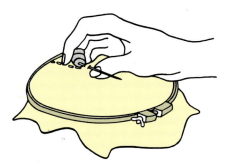

ROCKER QUILTING

This is the fastest, most accurate way of quilting. In rocker quilting, take several stitches on the needle before pulling it through the quilt layers. The smaller the stitches are the better your quilt will be, but this will depend on the pliability of the quilt. Do not attempt to take too many stitches on the needle at one time. This type of quilting always seems difficult at first but once you have set up a rhythm of upward and downward arcs it will be much easier. Keep your other hand under the work to check that the needle has passed through all the layers. The thread stitch can be very small and the fabric space slightly larger. This forms indentations which are responsible for the light and shade which give quilting its exciting dimensions.

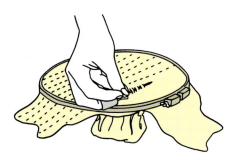

ADDITIONAL QUILTING STITCHES
Diagonal or lattice quilting with embroidery details
Diagonal lines can be stitched at regular intervals across the top of the design in one direction and then at the same intervals in the opposite direction to form a diamond pattern.

For a subtle effect, French knots can be worked at the intersections of the lattice. Another exciting idea is to work a small embroidered flower, such as a rosebud or forget-me-not, on the intersecting diagonals.

Back stitch
Back stitch (see page 92) gives a very strong quilting stitch and is particularly suitable for trapunto work.

Colonial knots
Colonial knots can also be used at regular intervals or at random to hold the textile sandwich together. If colonial knots (see page 102) are used as the quilting technique, the quilt will have to be lined on completion as these knots do not give the quilt a reversible back.

WHOLE-CLOTH QUILTS

This artistic form of quilting began hundreds of years ago in England and Wales. Made from one complete piece of fabric (usually monochrome and in fine, pure cotton) with no joins, the whole-cloth quilt was made using tiny quilting stitches which rely on the effect of light and shadow for the intrinsic design. The overall design was often complex, using a combination of many different quilting designs to create a coherent whole. Fully reversible, these quilts allowed the quilter to display his or her mastery of quilt design by using central medallions, filler quilting and detailed border designs.

It would be wise to make a *miniature* whole-cloth quilt so that you can perfect the quilting stitch and enjoy the experience of making a complete quilt in a limited time and at not too great an expense. Once you have made a miniature, you will feel confident enough to commit yourself to a full-scale whole-cloth quilt.

PREPARATION

Use a high-quality, pure cotton fabric and prewash it to avoid shrinkage and to wash out any excess dye or starch. Do not use the selvage. Use a thin, high-quality wadding, preferably with a warp and weft. Use the same fabric for the front and the backing or use a compatible backing.

TRANSFERRING THE QUILTING DESIGN

Once you have created or chosen your quilting design, transfer the design onto your fabric with a thin light line using one of the marking tools recommended on page 10. Remember to pretest the marker on a scrap of fabric to see that all the marks wash out. The marking line should not be visible once the quilt is complete.

Light-coloured fabric is easier to mark as the design can be traced directly onto the fabric. A light-table or a large window will help to highlight the design. Tape the design to the table or window and centre the quilt fabric over the design. Secure the quilt fabric with masking tape before tracing the entire design onto the whole cloth.

Quilting designs can be traced onto dark fabric by using dressmaker's carbon and a tracing wheel.

LAYERING THE QUILT AND TACKING

Prepare the textile sandwich (see page 26) and tack the top fabric, wadding and backing in radiating lines from the centre outwards.

Insert the quilt into a hoop or frame and, using a good quality quilting thread, work from the centre of the design outwards. Try rocker quilting (see page 28) to achieve a perfect stitch on both sides of the quilt. Keep the stitches as small as possible.

Once the quilting is complete, finish the quilt with a French binding (see page 60).

BELOW
Quilt artist: **Nanna van Rensburg**
Cross-hatch hand quilting enhanced by the addition of bullion knot flowers.

BOTTOM
Quilt artist: **Lesley Turpin-Delport**
Work in progress. A whole-cloth quilt design showing the many lanes of tacking required for a quilt which will be perfect on both sides.

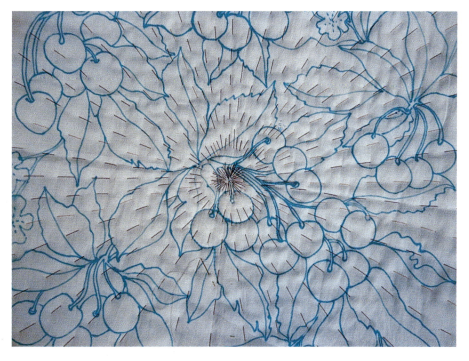

ABOVE
Quilt artist: **Sandi Lotter**
Machine pieced and machine quilted, this detail of a miniature friendship quilt shows the central area of the block that was originally designed for the signature of each friend.

RIGHT
Quilt artist: **Sandi Lotter**
Colorado star is a combination of log cabin and the eight-point star. Subtle colour choice with toning greys results in a central medallion shape. This machine-pieced quilt is now ready to be machine quilted.

OPPOSITE
Quilt artist: **Sandi Lotter**
A typical Amish doll holding her miniature rail fence quilt.

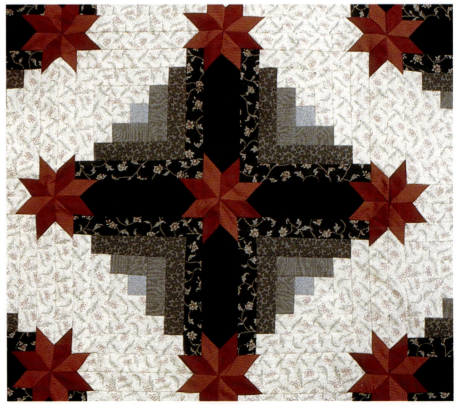

MACHINE QUILTING

Sandi Lotter, formerly of San Francisco, is an expert on machine quilting. She wants to make a lot of quilts in her lifetime and feels that machine quilting will allow her to make a number of 'quick quilts' with time for a few hand-pieced, hand-quilted ones in between. Sandi believes that there is a place for machine quilting. Not every quilt is meant to be a museum quality masterpiece. You may have taken a workshop to learn a specific technique and, while the resulting piece might not be perfect, it could become usable if quilted.

Wadding *(Batting)*

Sandi recommends four types of wadding for machine quilting: *Polyester wadding*, either bonded or unbonded, is ideal but it must not be too thick; *Mountain Mist* is the finest, softest polyester wadding that drapes well on a bed; *Loomtex wadding*, a bonded wadding which is ideal for wall hangings; and *cotton wadding*, which is best for an antique-look quilt because it shrinks when it is first washed. Cotton wadding must be quilted closely with the quilting lines no further than 3 cm (about 1 in) apart.

Thread

Use nylon thread for the top thread (clear for light-coloured quilts and smoky for a dark background) and 100% mercerized cotton for the bobbin.

Quilting designs *(stencils)*

Most designs can be adapted for machine quilting but a major requirement is that the design should be quilted in one continuous line. Play around with a design to see how you can adapt it to one continuous line.

TRANSFERRING THE DESIGN

Before sandwiching the quilt top to the wadding and lining, transfer the design onto the quilt top, using one of the methods recommended on page 10.

LAYERING THE QUILT AND PINNING

Lay out your lining (backing) fabric right side down, taping or clipping it to the working surface. Next, lay the wadding and then the quilt top (right side up) onto the lining to complete the textile sandwich (see page 26).

Using small safety pins, pin the three layers together, leaving no more than a flattened hand space between the pins.

HANDLING THE QUILT

When machine quilting, it is not necessary to start in the centre of the quilt as you do when hand quilting. When doing straight stitching (ditch or grid quilting – see below), sew one line of stitches from top to bottom (through the centre), then turn the quilt 90 degrees and repeat. You now have secured the top, wadding and lining.

Lay the quilt flat on the table or any large flat work surface and roll the quilt to the right of your first line of stitching as tightly as you possibly can towards the centre – until it is about 5 cm (2 in) from your quilting line. Now comes the secret ingredient – bicycle clips! Use the clips to secure the roll you have just made. Do the same with the left side. Now, stand at the bottom of the quilt (so that the rolls are on your left- and right-hand sides), and fold the quilt into a small, tight bundle. You can now begin quilting, working to your right. Unroll the right side, and re-roll the left side as you go along. Of course, if you are quilting a smaller piece (such as a crib quilt or wall hanging), you need not worry about the above ritual.

If you are doing free-motion quilting (see below), prepare the bundle as above, but instead of quilting all straight lines (as for grid or ditch), it is easier to work one complete block at a time. Quilt the block in the centre of the quilt first, then finish the remaining blocks in that row. Work to the right edge, unrolling the right side and re-rolling the left side as you go. Then turn the quilt 180 degrees and repeat. When doing free-motion quilting, many machine quilters find that it is easier first to do some ditch stitching around the blocks, as this helps to secure the top, wadding and lining to one another.

QUILTING OPTIONS

Sandi Lotter recommends the following three techniques for machine quilting.

Stitching in the ditch

This choice suits the walking-foot on your sewing machine. Use fairly long stitches and follow the design in your block by quilting in the seam lines. An example of this type of quilting can be seen on page 51 on the detail of the quilt entitled *Hidden Wells*.

Grid quilting

Sew straight lines one way and then the other way to form a grid. This type of design also suits the walking-foot.

Free-motion quilting

This is suitable for intricate designs such as feathers because the machinist is fully in control.

Set up your machine for free motion (darning mode) by dropping the feeding teeth (feed dog) and removing the pressure foot. Insert the fabric. Take one stitch manually, raise the needle and pull the bobbin thread through to the top, replace the needle in the same hole and begin sewing.

Make a few *really tiny stitches* to secure the quilting and then work slowly around your design in free straight stitch, trying to develop a rhythm. End with a few small stitches.

Continuous curve is another form of free-motion quilting. Plan your design so that you do not have to stop and start, twist or turn your fabric. Do not turn your work, but rather reverse quilt or move sideways.

Echo quilting follows the outline of the design at set intervals and is best done using free-motion quilting.

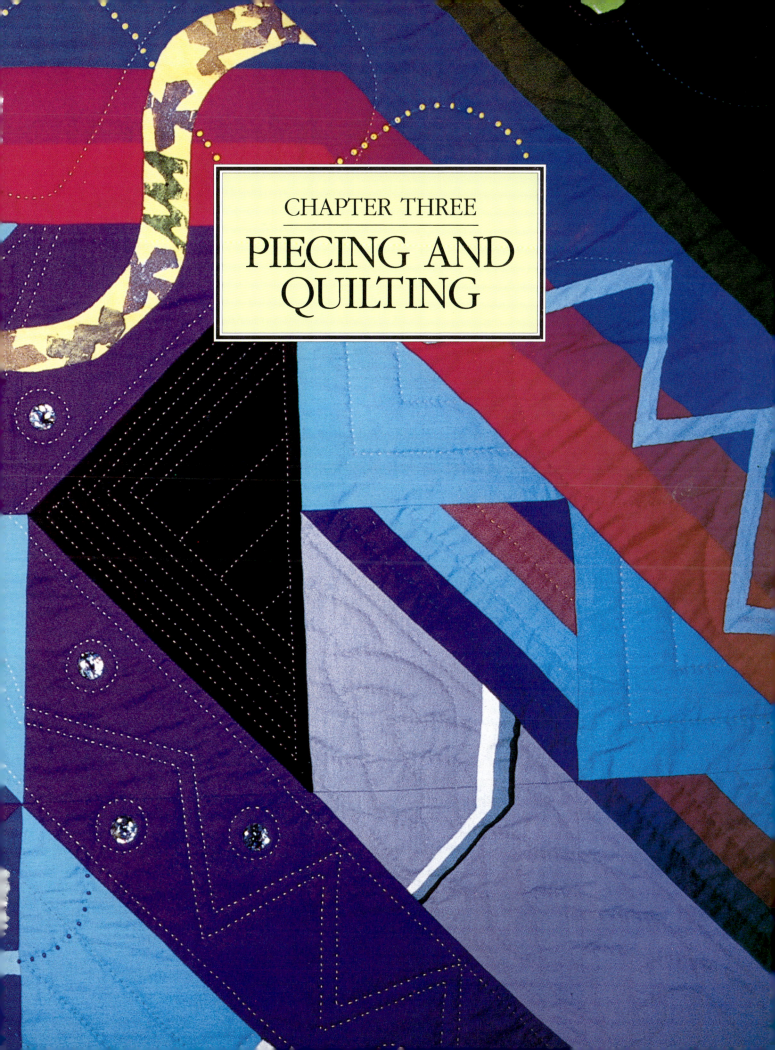

CHAPTER THREE
PIECING AND QUILTING

Patchwork is made by joining small patches of fabric together to make patterns. The geometric design which forms is the essential difference between appliqué and patchwork. The patches must be cut accurately and the fabric carefully planned. With clever placement of the patches and accurate joining, stunning results can be achieved.

The basic techniques described below will help you to create and experiment and make new quilts which could be the heirlooms of the future.

FABRIC
Fabric must be washable and colourfast. Choose finely woven fabrics, such as cotton, that fold easily. Avoid loosely woven fabrics which fray, stretch fabrics and synthetics. Sort the prints from the plain fabrics. Collect a selection of small, medium and large prints in colours ranging from light to dark. Fabrics should be of a similar type and preferably of the same weight.

Velvets, linens and silks should only be used by advanced patchwork artists, as these fabrics are difficult to handle.

Colours can be boldly contrasting or subtly shaded. Choose a basic pattern and work out the colour scheme. Begin by making a small piece of patchwork, and master the basics before tackling patchwork that is more adventurous.

TEMPLATES
Templates must be made for each pattern piece in the block. Make these from cardboard, sandpaper or old X-ray plate. Sharp scissors, pencil, graph paper, set-square, ruler, protractor and a pair of compasses are essential equipment.

Draw the template shape on graph paper or simply trace a template directly from this book, and cut it out. Place the paper template on the cardboard, trace around it and cut it out accurately. Three types of template can be used:

Single template
This is made the exact size of the finished patch. A 6 mm (¼ in) seam allowance is then added to the fabric.

Two templates
One, the size of the finished patch, is used for the backing paper and the other, which includes the seam allowance, is used for the fabric patch.

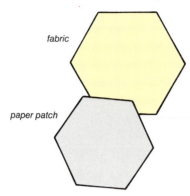

Window template
This template is an empty frame: the inner edge is the size of the backing paper and the outer edge the size of the fabric patch with the seam allowance included.

NOTE: *Stamps, used with an ink pad, are commercially available for marking the template shape directly onto the wrong side of your fabric.*

BASIC SHAPES
Most designs are based on the square which can be divided into triangles, rectangles and more squares. These basic shapes used in different proportions and combinations give rise to new geometric shapes, such as diamonds, parallelograms and trapezoids.

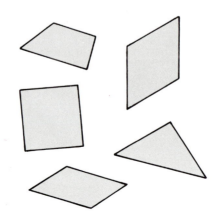

Other designs are based on the circle, or parts of the circle, to produce polygons. Curved shapes are very difficult to piece together so they are usually hand pieced, or appliquéd to square patches which are then pieced together.

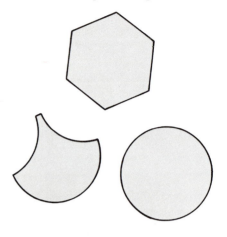

PREPARING THE PATCHES
The purists believe that the most accurate patchwork is achieved with paper backings (typing paper is ideal) and hand patching, especially for hexagons and curved shapes.

Paper backing or in-lay method
1. *Place the template on the paper, draw around the shape with a pencil and cut the paper as accurately as possible. The backing paper must be the exact size of the finished patch.*

2. *For the fabric patches, place the template on the wrong side of the fabric with one edge exactly on the grain line, parallel to the selvage. Draw around the template, remembering to add the 6 mm (¼ in) seam allowance unless it has already been incorporated into the template.*

3. *Cut pieces patch by patch for accuracy and then sort the patches according to colour and shape.*

4. *Pin a paper patch to the wrong side of each fabric patch.*

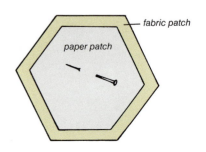

5. *Fold the fabric edges over to the exact size of the paper and tack them in position. Press the folds.*

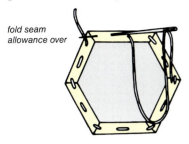

With triangular and diamond shapes, fold the edges to form sharp points.

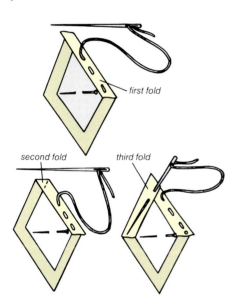

Piecing by hand

For circles and curved shapes, tack around the fabric edges first. Place the paper patch in the centre of the fabric and pull the tacking thread gently until the circle fits the paper patch. Make a back stitch and cut off the thread.

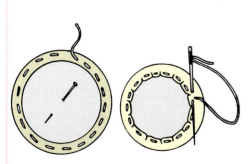

6. *Now the patches can be pieced together to form blocks.*

PIECING THE PATCHES

Piecing is the process of sewing all the small patchwork pieces together by hand or machine. The type of patchwork and the shapes used will determine which method of joining is best.

Piecing by hand

The paper-backed fabric patches must be sewn together with small, evenly spaced overcasting stitches. These stitches must be as invisible as possible. Join the patches in blocks, in rows or in one continuous piece.

Each block must make one complete pattern. Attach the blocks to each other in rows.

When all the rows have been completed, whip stitch them together with right sides facing. Iron the completed work and then remove the tacking and paper patches.

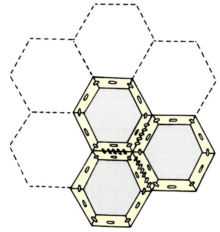

Joining hexagons in blocks

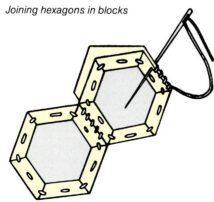

Joining hexagons in rows

Although this method is slow, it is very accurate and has the advantage of allowing the quilter to lay out the design before joining the patches and changing or redesigning the shapes which do not work.

Patchwork shapes can also be pieced together without the use of backing paper, as described below.

Single-seam method (American)

Place the fabric pieces right sides together and join them with small even running stitches, beginning with a knot and a back stitch and ending with a back stitch or a double stitch and a knot. Remember to maintain a perfect seam allowance of 6 mm (¼ in). Press all the seams open or to one side. The single seam can also be machine stitched.

NOTE: *The running stitch can have an occasional back stitch included for extra strength.*

Quilt artist: **Pat Perry**
Detail of a traditional, hand-pieced quilt (top), using the paper-backed method. The paper-backed patches are clearly visible (bottom).

OPPOSITE
Quilt Artist: **Julia Clephane**
The balance of cool and warm colours shows a progression from the basic cube (tumbling block) to the more complex inner city block. Julia tests her design by pinning the shapes to a styrofoam board as the design develops.

ABOVE
Quilt artist: **Adrienne Yates**
Little Red School House is a traditional block which lends itself to hand piecing with paper backings. Notice the embroidery details on the windows.

RIGHT
Quilt artist: **Margee Gough**
Machine and hand piecing have been used in this advanced sampler *David's Star*. Notice the different quilting techniques used to define each block.

37

ABOVE
Quilt artist: **Margee Gough**
Based on two different blocks, namely *February's Finest* and *Norwegian Wood*, this quilt is entitled *Strawberry Fields* and is hand pieced with machine-sewn borders.

LEFT
Quilt artist: **Jessica van Niekerk**
Hand pieced and hand quilted, this quilt uses hexagons and the six-point star combined in a medallion layout.

OPPOSITE
Each block of this *pineapple* friendship quilt was machine pieced by members of a quilters' group and then hand quilted by Isabel Scott. The detail shows the strength of the black strips which dominate the pineapple design. The block is traditional but three colour ways have been used per block which accounts for the interesting diagonal pull. The black shapes rotate in a circular motion, giving an illusion of interlocking cog wheels.

PIECING BY MACHINE

Machine stitching is excellent for patchwork pieces with long, straight sides but is not recommended for curved patches.

With right sides together, machine straight stitch the fabric, maintaining a 6 mm (¼ in) seam allowance.

Join the patches in rows and iron the seams open and flat or to one side. Join the rows together to form blocks.

One patchwork design that is ideal for machine piecing is the log cabin (see page 156 for templates).

Log cabin (Fold over) patchwork

This design is worked in square blocks composed of half light and half dark strips that are stitched and folded around a small centre square.

A foundation square of calico (the size of the finished block) gives strength to the patchwork and acts as a guide when positioning the strips. The disadvantage of a foundation square is the extra bulk which hampers quilting and adds weight to the quilt. Once you have mastered the log cabin method, however, you can omit the foundation square, but then the seam lines must be marked on each piece of fabric to ensure accuracy.

TRADITIONAL LOG CABIN METHOD

1. *Fold and press two diagonal lines from corner to corner on the calico square to help you position the strips.*

2. *Cut out the small centre square (template on page 156) and pin it to the foundation (calico) square.*

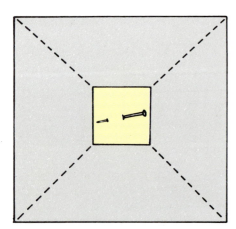

3. *Using templates 1 and 2, cut out pieces in dark fabrics.*

4. *Place strip 1 face down over the centre square. Machine straight stitch through all the layers 6 mm (¼ in) from the edge. Fold back the strip and press.*

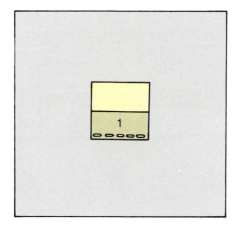

5. *Secure strip 2 in the same way.*

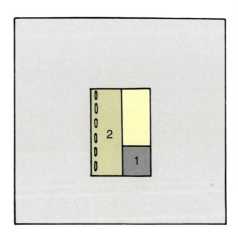

6. *Cut strips in light fabric using templates 3 and 4. Secure and fold these light strips in the same way. The first circuit is now complete.*

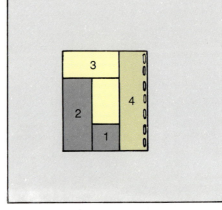

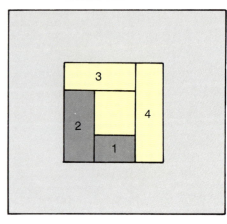

7. *Continue securing the strips in the same way, maintaining light and dark patterning throughout.*

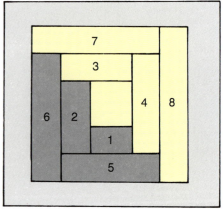

8. *When the required number of blocks have been made, join them in rows, right sides together, and stitch with a 6 mm (¼ in) seam allowance.*

9. *Prepare the fabric for quilting (see page 26) and quilt the patchwork by stitching along the seams of each strip to form radiating squares, or by stitching on the diagonals.*

NOTE: *The light and dark halves of the block form different variations of the log cabin pattern, depending on how they are positioned, for example medallions, open diamonds, diagonals, zigzags and windmills. Variations can also be achieved by attaching the strips in different ways, like the 'Pineapple' design (see page 52), and 'Hidden Wells' (see page 50), both of which use the strip cutting and piecing method described on page 46.*

Quilt artist: **Jolena van Rooyen**
This log cabin quilt was made using the paper-piecing method (see page 54) for accurate piecing in the machine. This quilt won first prize in the log cabin section at a national quilt festival in 1987.

ABOVE
Quilt artist: **Jolena van Rooyen**
An original design by Jolena, this concept begins with a curved triangle as the centre. Strips cut on the bias are then placed around this centre triangle. The design has been worked in three different colours, ranging from light to dark. Once again, a paper foundation has been used for accurate machine piecing.

RIGHT
Quilt artist: **Adrienne Yates**
Although traditional in layout, this quilt has been made up from *torn* strips of fabric in lightweight wools and cottons.

OPPOSITE
Quilt artist: **Ettie Muter**
Peacock fantasia is a chevron design based on the log cabin. The central square in each diamond gives the illusion of the 'eye' of the peacock feather.

OPPOSITE
Quilt artist: **Anne van der Riet**
This is a wonderfully modern interpretation of the traditional cathedral window design. Warm pinks are toned down by areas of blue and a striking focal point is achieved with the yellow and turquoise square.

RIGHT
Quilt artist: **Susan Sittig**
The plain, bright colours used in this machine-pieced, hand-quilted work create marvellous optical vibrations.

BELOW RIGHT
Quilt artist: **Sabera Sarang**
Machine-pieced and hand-quilted *Swirling ribbons* employs the full colour spectrum: primary and secondary colours; tints and tones.

BELOW
Quilt artist: **Annetjie Taute**
Primary colours and simple shapes produce this striking and easy-to-make machine-pieced quilt entitled *Boats*.

STRIP PIECING

Clever quilters have come up with exciting and innovative methods of speeding up the cutting process and making the piecing more accurate. Instead of cutting each piece of patchwork, long strips of fabric are cut to the desired width and length using a rotary cutter and plastic strips.

The strips of fabric are sewn together by machine to create the fabric from which the quilt surface will be designed. The shapes are marked with a ruler and pencil or with a template and then cut from the strip-pieced meterage. The shapes are then re-sewn to create a complete quilt surface.

REQUIREMENTS
Sewing machine: clean and well oiled.
Sharp new needle.
Thread: good quality sewing-machine thread to suit your fabric choice.
Scissors: a pair each for fabric and paper plus a small, sharp-pointed pair.
Rotary cutter and a cutting board (Teflon).
A set of perspex strips of different widths.
Quilter's rulers (optional): special rulers are available from specialist quilting shops for a number of different designs, for example Margaret le Roux's quilter's companion, pineapple ruler, squares, triangles and diamonds and quilter's quarter.
Marking pencils: a selection of graphite pencils (HB, 2B), or chalk.
Equipment for templates: cutting knife; squared paper (for squares, rectangles and triangles); isometric paper for diamonds, hexagons and cubes; cardboard or transparent plastic for templates.
Fabric: 100% pure cotton in different colours and patterns.
Iron for pressing the seams.

The technique
MARKING AND CUTTING THE STRIPS
The marking and cutting of the strips must be done carefully and accurately or the design will not match up.

1. *Decide on the size of your strips. Strips should not be cut longer than 1.4 m (1.5 yds) for large projects and although strips can be any width, they should not be cut narrower than 2 cm (¾ in) in order to accommodate the seam allowance. The strips can be cut across the grain (that is from selvage to selvage). As a guide, the strips should be scaled to the size of the shape that will be cut from them, as well as to the size of your quilt.*

2. *Mark a series of points the required width apart and join these points with your ruler. The width must include seam allowances, that is 6 mm (¼ in) on each side. Mark off as many strips as required along the length of the fabric.*

You can use perspex strips as templates and pencil the cutting line directly onto the fabric (the perspex strip must include seam allowance). Using the rotary cutter, cut along the pencil lines to form strips.

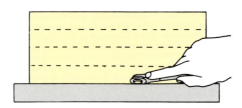

JOINING THE STRIPS
1. *Pin two strips, right sides together, at regular intervals.*

2. *Set your seam allowance of 6 mm (¼ in) and begin machine stitching, guiding the fabric with both hands and maintaining a perfect seam allowance.*

3. *Join the required number of strips and press the seams. The ultimate design will determine how the seam allowances are ironed. Simple strip piecing can have the seams ironed open and flat, while other designs require ironing all the seams in one direction or towards the dark fabrics. The best way to iron is to minimize the bulk of the seam allowance when the blocks are joined.*

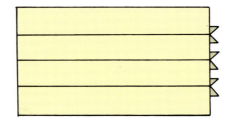

NOTE: *When joining the strips, use the presser foot of your sewing machine as your guide for the seam allowance. Alternatively, stick double-sided adhesive (mirror) tape to the machine plate to create a ridge. When sewing, the fabric butts against the tape, keeping the seam allowance accurate.*

You will have to experiment and create a block or part of your design to assess how much fabric you will need.

4. *If a number of sets of strips are needed, chain sew the sets, cutting the thread between the sets at the end.*

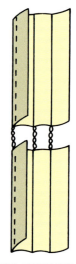

MARKING AND CUTTING THE DESIGN TEMPLATES
Mark the shape required on the strip-pieced fabric with pencil and cut out the basic shapes, for example squares, triangles or random shapes.

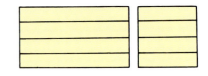

Square

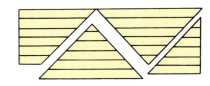

Triangle

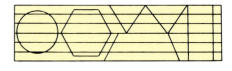

Random shapes

RIGHT
Quilt artist: **Annamarie Ankerman**
Orion is a fine example of the effective use of strip piecing combined with hand quilting and appliquéd beading.

BELOW
Quilt artist: **Gerda Klaasen**
Strip piecing and the clever use of colour combine to produce the masculine lines in *Roman stripe* (Amish design).

BASIC NINE-PATCH QUILT
Certain Amish quilts, the *Radiant Nine-Patch Quilt*, which is described in full on page 64, and *Hidden Wells* (page 50) use the quick strip-piecing method.

REQUIREMENTS
Fabrics: about 25 cm (10 in) in two different colours will be plenty to enable you to experiment and become familiar with the cutting and piecing technique.
5 cm (2 in) wide perspex strip.
Rotary cutter and cutting board.

MARKING AND CUTTING THE STRIPS
1. Iron the first 25 cm (10 in) piece of fabric on the wrong side using a spray starch. (The spray starch is optional but it does keep the fabric from shifting when being cut.) Turn the fabric right side up and place the second colour down on it, right sides together. Spray starch and iron again.

2. Using your perspex strip and rotary cutter on a Teflon board, cut at least three 5 cm (2 in) wide strips, from selvage to selvage through both layers.

JOINING THE STRIPS
1. Set the pairs of strips to one side.

2. Take one set and sew the first pair of strips together (first colour on top) with a slightly bigger than usual seam allowance of 8 mm (⁵⁄₁₆ in). This will give a finished block of about 10 cm (4 in).

3. Without cutting the sewing thread, chain sew the next pair of strips so that the second colour is on top.

4. Now take a strip of the first colour and join it to the second colour on the first pair of strips (you will now have three strips joined together).

5. Now join the third strip (second colour) to the first colour on the second pair of strips. You will now have three strips joined together in opposite colour combinations.

6. Iron the seam allowance towards the darker colour.

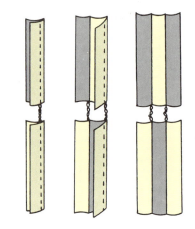

MARKING AND CUTTING THE PIECED STRIPS
1. Place the two opposite sets, right sides together, ready for cutting. Once you are experienced at cutting, you will be able to cut a couple of layers at the same time.

2. Use your 5 cm (2 in) perspex strip and cut through all the layers to make a series of strips each 5 cm (2 in) wide.

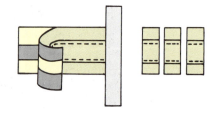

3. Stack strips at right angles to one another.

JOINING STRIPS TO FORM THE NINE-PATCH BLOCK
1. Machine two strips together and continue chain sewing these first sets together, but turning each alternate set so that the opposite fabric combination is on top.

2. Now add the third section to each set to make up the nine-patch block. Chain sew this last section, remembering to alternate the top section.

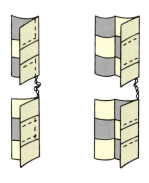

3. Cut the machine threads to separate the blocks and press the seams towards the greater number of dark squares. You should have two different nine-patch blocks: Block A with 5 dark squares and 4 light squares and Block B with 5 light squares and 4 dark.

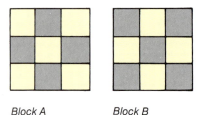

Block A   Block B

The original strips of fabric (that is, three strips of each colour cut 5 cm (2 in) from selvage to selvage) should make about 12 to 14 blocks.

OPPOSITE
Quilt artist: **Lesley Turpin-Delport**
A detail of *Philip's Radiant Nine-patch* quilt (see page 64) showing the arrangement of the blocks.

ABOVE
Quilt artist: **Margee Gough**
Margee has used the basic nine-patch in her Amish quilt but has made it even more interesting by adding a shocking pink centre. This quilt measures 160 x 160 cm (63 x 63 in) and has been machine pieced using hand-dyed fabric. Notice the clever use of cross-hatch and feather quilting.

HIDDEN WELLS

An exciting and innovative use of strip piecing is seen in Margee Gough's *Hidden Wells Quilt*, which is based on a concept introduced by Mary Ellen Hopkins.

This design looks like a very clever log cabin combination, but is in fact an advanced design based on strips of fabric pieced together, cut into triangles and re-assembled to give a balance of horizontals versus verticals. It is the juggling of the re-assembled squares that accounts for the exciting optical illusions.

If you are apprehensive about making this design, try a mock-up by cutting strips of fabric and glueing them to a piece of paper. Follow the instructions below and you will be astounded with the results.

REQUIREMENTS

Nine different colour-coordinated fabrics. This particular quilt has nine fabrics, but you can use from five to nine. To get good contrasting squares, take two basic colours (for example blue and yellow) and put all the blues at the top and all the yellows at the bottom.

Fabric for the borders. (Choose this fabric only after you have joined the squares so that you can see which colours will be most suitable.)

METHOD

1. Using the nine different fabrics, cut a strip along the width of each piece of fabric. Cut each of the nine strips with a different width, making two strips particularly different from the rest (that is, one is very narrow and one very wide. As these two strips will form the top and bottom of the squares in the design they must contrast in width, colour and fabric).

2. Sew the strips together lengthwise in pairs and press open the seams.

3. Sew the pairs of strips together until all the strips have been joined, making sure that the two contrasting strips lie at the top and bottom of the pieced strip.

NOTE: Once joined, the strips used in the quilt illustrated opposite should measure 17.8 cm (7 in). When re-assembled (see step 6), the squares should then measure 13 cm (5 in).

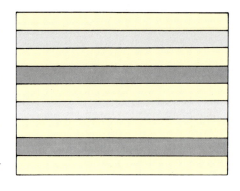

4. Measure the width of the completed strip and, using a set square, cut the strip accurately into eight squares. (When re-assembled, these eight squares will give you 16 smaller squares – see step 6.)

5. Now cut each square on both diagonals to create four new triangles. It is vitally important to number these triangles as they form the basis of four basic blocks. Use small adhesive stickers and number them 1 to 4 as shown in the illustration. (You should have eight No. 1s, eight No. 2s, eight No. 3s and eight No. 4s)

6. With right sides together, sew triangle No. 1 to triangle No. 3 to form Square A; No. 1 to No. 4 to form Square B; No. 2 to No. 3 to form Square C and No. 2 to No. 4 to form Square D. (You should now have four As, four Bs, four Cs and four Ds.)

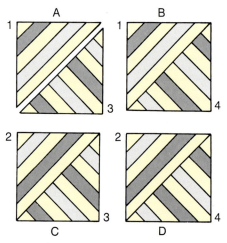

7. Now re-group and sew the four small blocks to form brand new blocks about 25 cm (10 in) square. (Label two of them Block I and two Block II.)

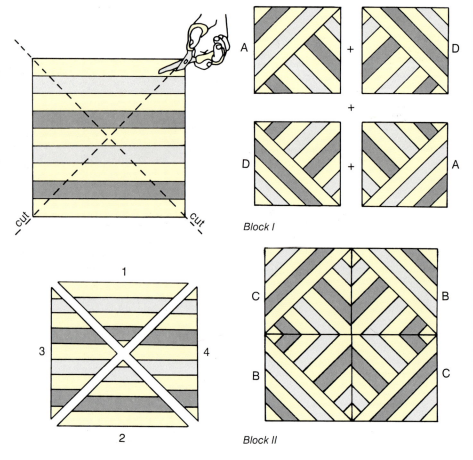

Block I

Block II

NOTE: *When joining the As to the Ds and the Bs to the Cs, check that the four centre triangles with the nine vertical strips all meet in the middle.*

8. *Now assemble the new large blocks in opposite pairs to form the squares within squares which is the essence of Hidden Wells.*

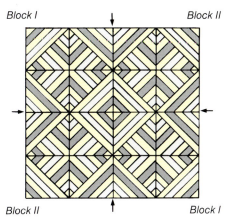

Block I　　　　　　　Block II

Block II　　　　　　　Block I

9. *Repeat steps 1 to 8 to make up more big blocks (the quilt depicted consists of 20 blocks), then join them in sets of blocks until the measurement suits your quilt top.*

10. *Attach the borders as described on page 60. In the quilt shown opposite, the quilt artist used two simple borders about 7.5 cm (3 in) wide with mitred corners, then a strip-pieced border 9 cm (3½ in) wide and finally a plain border 13 cm (5 in) wide. The latter two borders were both attached with straight corners.*

11. *Prepare the quilt for quilting (see page 26) and quilt each square down the centre of each strip to give the illusion of each strip being double.*

12. *If using the same borders as used by the quilt artist, quilt the plain borders with a cable design (see page 129) and the pieced border in the ditch (see page 31).*

Quilt artist: **Margee Gough**
Although *Hidden Wells* looks like a very clever log cabin combination, this design is based on strips of fabric pieced together, cut into triangles and re-assembled to give a balance of horizontals versus verticals.

51

PINEAPPLE LOG CABIN

Once you have grasped the principles of strip cutting and a paper foundation, try a miniature in patchwork.

The pineapple design is probably the most complex of the log cabin variations but, although difficult to plan and assemble, the effect is stunning, full of motion and excitement.

The example of the *Pineapple Log Cabin* shown opposite is a miniature quilt, which takes greater dexterity, as the seam allowances are so small: 3 mm (⅛ in), instead of the normal 6 mm (¼ in). However, strip piecing and a paper foundation make the job easier.

The pineapple design is based on an eight-sided figure. Strips of one value (cream calico) are sewn around the centre square on each of the four sides on the horizontal/vertical plane while strips of contrasting value (blue fabric) are sewn on the four sides of the diagonal plane. The same value must be maintained on the same plane throughout.

If you make one block before planning the miniature quilt, this will give you an idea of how much fabric you will need for each block.

REQUIREMENTS

Navy and burgundy fabric for the centre piece and corner strips.
Cream calico for the horizontal and vertical strips.
At least four shades of blue fabric for the diagonal strips.
Blue sprig fabric for the borders and navy and burgundy fabric for the French binding.

METHOD

1. Using the navy and burgundy fabric, cut out your 2.5 cm (1 in) centre square [1.9 cm (¾ in) plus 6 mm (¼ in) for the seam allowance].

2. Using the cream calico, cut out 1.6 cm (⅝ in) wide strips along the width of the fabric.

3. Using the five blue fabrics, cut out 1.6 cm (⅝ in) wide strips along the width of each fabric.

4. Enlarge the template given below to measure 11 cm (4 in) and make a copy of it on a piece of paper.

5. Pin the navy and burgundy centre square to the paper foundation.

6. *Using a 3 mm (⅛ in) seam allowance, sew on the first two strips of calico and press them back as shown.*

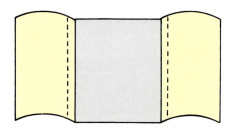

7. *Using the paper foundation as a guide, cut each calico strip to form a triangle.*

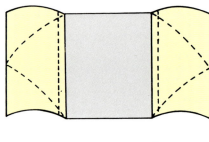

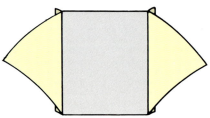

8. *Sew on the top and bottom horizontal calico strips, pressing them back and cutting them to form triangles.*

9. *Cut the tip off each triangle to form trapezoids.*

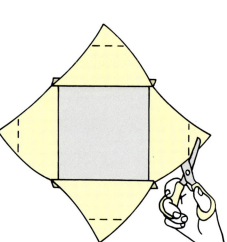

10. *Using the paper foundation as a guide, sew the fabric strips from the blue range on diagonally, across the intersections of the first row of calico strips as shown.*

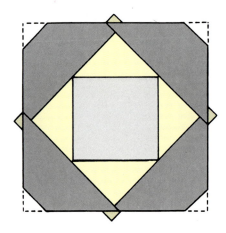

11. *Press back the four strips and, using the template as a guide, cut them into triangles.*

12. *Cut the tips off each triangle to form trapezoids.*

13. *Repeat the calico fabric strips on the horizontal and vertical planes.*

14. *Continue repeating the same value fabric on the same plane (that is, blue on the diagonal and calico on the horizontal and vertical planes) until the paper foundation is covered.*

15. *For the corners, use wider strips (3.5 cm/1⅜ in) in the same fabric as the centre square, sewing them on diagonally and pressing them back as before.*

16. *Using a set square, trim off the excess fabric to form a perfect square the size of the paper foundation, 11 cm (4 in).*

17. *Remove the paper foundation carefully. It is very important that you do not jerk or tear the paper roughly as this may loosen the stitches.*

18. *Repeat steps 1 to 17, using a variety of blue/calico combinations until you have 16 miniature pineapple blocks (that is, 4 x 4 blocks).*

19. *Sew the completed blocks together in rows and, using one of the blue sprig fabrics, attach the border (see page 60).*

20. *Prepare the quilt for quilting (see page 26) and quilt in the ditch (see page 31) around the basic block and with zigzag quilting along the sprigged border.*

21. *Finally, complete the quilt by sewing on navy and burgundy French binding as shown on page 60.*

Quilt artist: **Margee Gough**
This miniature quilt measures just 40 cm (15¾ in) square. In this variation of log cabin, the calico strips are sewn on horizontally and vertically around a navy and burgundy central square while blue patterned strips are sewn on the four sides of the diagonal plane. Notice how the navy and burgundy fabric has been used at the corners of each block and create a diamond pattern once the blocks are pieced together.

KALEIDOSCOPE QUILT

Having looked at strip piecing, another modern approach to quick and accurate piecing is the use of a photocopy machine. The speed of this machine, and the fact that many designs can be run off and cut up into templates, has promoted the idea of the quilter being able to test the layout of a design by making a number of photocopies of a block and juggling the blocks to produce the most pleasing design. Templates can be glued onto cardboard and a patch of sandpaper attached to the back so that the templates do not slip on the fabric.

Once a design has been formulated, the basic block can be photocopied a number of times and used as a paper foundation for accurate piecing by different members of a quilt group.

Jolena van Rooyen is an expert and calls her technique the quick 'paper-piecing' method. Jolena is a mathematician and a quiltmaker who has won top honours at Quilt Festivals and has also acted as a judge at competitions.

Here are Jolena's instructions for making her *Kaleidoscope Quilt*.

REQUIREMENTS
Basic sewing requirements (see page 10).
Magic tape.
A quick unpick (or seam ripper) for removing the paper.
Typing paper for the template.
Fabric: about 10 different sprigged cotton fabrics in light, medium and dark colours.

NOTE: *Set yourself up with your sewing machine placed on a towel folded double so that the towel drops down in front of the work surface, leaving a small space in front of the machine for ironing. Set up an ironing board next to your seat at the same height as your work surface. Place the iron next to your machine as most of the ironing is done on the towel. The board is used for long seams only.*

METHOD

1. Trace the kaleidoscope template (see page 152) onto typing paper. Calculate the number of blocks that you will need for your quilt top.

Notice that a dotted line is drawn 6 mm (¼ in) on either side of the solid line (joining line) and that each part is numbered in the joining sequence.

2. Make a photocopy of each block needed for the quilt. These are your foundation papers.

NOTE: *Check that the photocopies do not distort the original.*

3. Make two templates (see page 152) for the fabrics, adding 8 mm (⅓ in) all round for the seam allowance. This larger-than-usual seam is later trimmed to 6 mm (¼ in).

4. Place the templates on the fabric and cut as many layers as possible together, as the accuracy comes in the piecing rather than the cutting. Check that the templates are aligned with the grain of the fabric (straight grain, parallel to the selvage).

5. On a separate piece of paper or tray, arrange the pieces of fabric for the first block, following the template.

6. Cut the first photocopy diagonally, as shown below. Turn the photocopy over and place fabric piece No. 1 in position with the wrong side of the fabric against the photocopy. The light of the machine will show up the lines. With right sides together, place fabric piece No. 2 on fabric piece No. 1. Pin well.

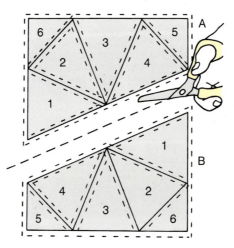

7. Turn the photocopy over and sew through the paper on the line between 1 and 2. Make a double stitch at the beginning and end of each seam. This is necessary for extra strength as the seam must hold when the paper foundation is torn away.

8. Sew fabric No. 3 to fabric No. 2 in a similar way. Continue to No. 6.

9. Check every time that each piece fits perfectly, then trim the stitched seam to 6 mm (¼ in), fold the seams open and press.

10. Sew the other half of the block in the same way.

NOTE: *If the paper tears while working, use Magic tape to repair the damage.*

11. Aligning the centre and edges, pin, then sew the two halves together. Press open the seam.

12. Repeat steps 5 to 11 until you have the required number of blocks for your quilt. Sew the blocks in rows and then join the rows together, sewing on the lines provided by the photocopies. Press well, and then sew on the borders (see page 60).

13. Now remove the paper carefully. Do not jerk or tear roughly or the stitching may come loose.

14. Prepare the quilt for quilting (see page 26). Quilt as desired, then attach the binding (see page 60).

NOTE: *If this technique appears difficult, try to make one block first and then make photocopies of the block to calculate how many blocks you will need and to help you with colour combinations. Most photocopy machines will give an adequate reproduction if you place the fabric directly on the glass screen of the photocopy machine.*

OPPOSITE
Quilt artist: **Jolena van Rooyen**
This talented quilt artist uses the quick 'paper-piecing' method in which a template is photocopied for each block in the quilt and the fabric patches sewn onto the paper foundation to ensure accurate piecing. The *Kaleidoscope* quilt shown opposite is an example of what can be achieved using this unique technique. This quilt is also a scrap quilt made from all Jolena's leftover bits and pieces. The fabrics are all floral. The central area is predominantly dark red, orange and rust contrasting with the adjacent blues, golds and pink tones. The black background in the border fabric provides a strong frame for the quilt top.

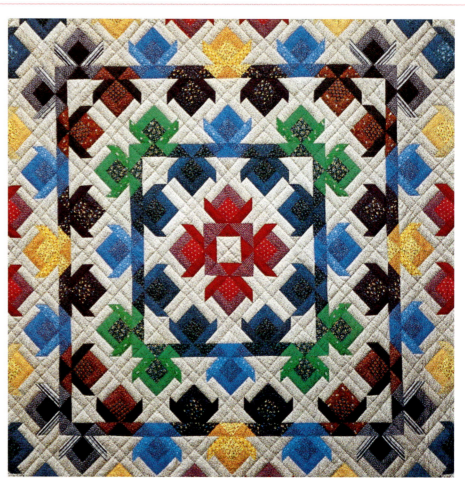

Maretha Fourie is a true innovator in the piecing world, having designed and incorporated the protea motif into traditional quilting concepts. A home economics and art history graduate, she acquired a masters degree in clothing textiles and related arts in the United States.

Quilts made by Maretha's Protea House Group have been exhibited in Canberra and Sydney in Australia; in the Museum das Artes de Sao Paolo in Brazil and in Monte Video, Uraguay. Another of her protea designs was presented to the Pope in 1982.

FAR OPPOSITE
Quilt artist: **June Kruger**
The quilting patterns in the proteas designed by Maretha Fourie account for the tactile quality of the shapes. Notice the excellent choice of border fabrics.

TOP OPPOSITE
Quilt artist: **Maretha Fourie**
An exquisite example of *Protea caffra* designed by Maretha.

BELOW OPPOSITE
Quilt artist: **Maretha Fourie**
Another example of a protea design by Maretha Fourie, this time a detail of *Protea rubropilosa*.

ABOVE RIGHT
Quilt artist: **Suzette Ehlers**
Detail of one of Maretha Fourie's original protea designs constructed by Suzette Ehlers. The protea design is complemented by the block set on point while the border pattern contains the design within a frame.

RIGHT
Quilt artist: **Joey McDonald (Golden Rand Guild)**
An original Maretha Fourie design. Notice the exciting quilting patterns in the corner areas.

AFRO-AMERICAN QUILTS

And now for something completely different!

Afro-American quilts originated from the 'throw-together' quilts that Negro slaves made, after work, to provide warm covers for cold winter nights. Rumour has it that the Negro slaves were not allowed scissors, which were regarded as weapons, so they had to tear the fabric to make their patches. This possibly accounts for the irregularity of the traditional blocks that they used. Although the Negro women made these quilts from necessity, there is a pleasing creativity in the haphazard way the traditional blocks were put together.

These quilts were made from whatever fabric scraps were available and as quickly as possible. The scraps were patched into long, narrow strips that were then stitched together to make the quilt top.

The name 'Afro-American' comes from the similarity between these patched quilts and the fabrics from Africa that were first woven in long, narrow strips and then seamed together to make yards of cloth.

If you like the idea of making a quilt which blends the cultures of Africa and America, try the following ideas to create your own haphazard Afro-American quilt:

Choose a simple, traditional pattern. The dominant colours are usually yellow, red and turquoise. Make up the quilt from about nine blocks. The block size can vary from 20 cm (8 in) to 30 cm (12 in), which will give the quilt its lopsided quality. Although the design consists of one basic block, you should try to make each block *look* different. In other words, there should be no symmetry.

The following tips will give you some ideas for changing the basic block:

❏ Make the same block but change the *size* of the square
❏ Make the same block but change the *proportion* of the parts within the square
❏ Draw the design *freehand* and then cut it out
❏ Use the same block in *different fabrics*
❏ Make the same block, and *leave out one part*
❏ Make a block using *horizontal strips of fabric*
❏ Design a block with *long, vertical strips of fabric*
❏ Make a block where the *fabric dominates* the basic design
❏ To provide an element of surprise, *change the design* altogether
❏ Sew on the blocks horizontally, adding in sashing (see page 16) where necessary. The borders do not have to match, the back of the quilt can also be pieced, and the outer binding does not have to match the basic block.

ABOVE
Quilt artist: **Sally Scott**
Warm ochres contrast with patterned and plain blocks in this example of the haphazard Afro-American quilt.

OPPOSITE
Quilt artist: **Jeanette Gilks**
Jeanette has used five permutations of 'a diamond in the square': original colour; new colour; the block reduced to a quarter; a section of the existing block enlarged, and an alien block.

FINISHING YOUR PIECED QUILT

When all the blocks have been assembled, either by hand or machine, the patched fabric must be quilted (see Chapter Two) and finished. Fancy borders incorporating patterns from the main design can be added or the quilt can be edged with fabric binding as described below.

BORDERS
How to assemble the borders and finish corners

The width and length of your borders will depend on the size of the centre piece and your design plan (see borders on page 17). Add 6 mm (¼ in) seam allowances to the border strips.

There are three basic corners: the *straight corner*, the *straight corner with a block* and the *mitred corner*.

I have chosen the Amish layout to show the construction of a straight corner, and the straight corner with a block.

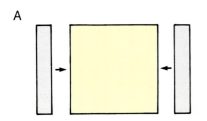

A

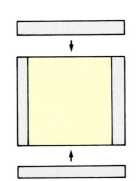

B

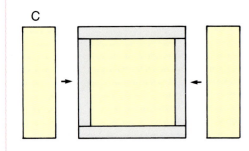

C

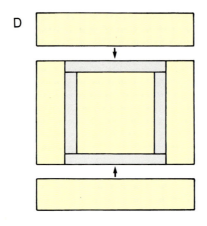

D

Straight corner

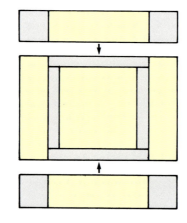

Straight corner with a block

MAKING A MITRED CORNER:
1. *Measure the length of the sides of the centre piece and add twice the width of the border strip. Cut out the two side strips.*

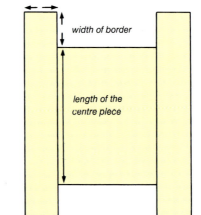

2. *Sew these two borders to the quilt top, stopping and starting 6 mm (¼ in) away from the corners.*

3. *Now measure the length of the remaining sides, add on twice the width measurement of the border and cut out the two horizontal border strips.*

4. *Sew on these two strips, stopping 6 mm (¼ in) from the corners.*

5. *Now fold and crease the ends at 45 degrees. Mark this diagonal and sew the border strips together on the line, working from the outside corners inwards towards the quilt. Check that the corner is correct, and then trim off the excess fabric.*

6. *Press the seams open and flat.*

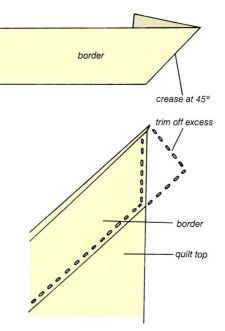

COMPLETING THE EDGES
Added binding *(French binding)*
The binding of a quilt should be strong and it should complement the quilt top.

1. *Once all the quilting has been completed, tack along the outside edges of the textile sandwich. Leaving a 6 mm (¼ in) seam allowance, trim the edges with scissors or a rotary cutter so that the edges of all three layers are even.*

2. *Cut bindings about 9 cm (3½ in) in width for large quilts and about 4.5 cm (1¾ in) for miniature quilts. The binding must be cut on the straight grain for straight edges and on the cross (bias) for curved edges.*

3. *Fold the binding in half lengthwise and iron to secure your fold.*

4. *With right sides together, position the raw edge of the binding on the edge of the quilted top. Machine or hand stitch the binding to the quilt edge, approximately 6 mm (¼ in) from the outer raw edges.*

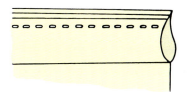

5. *Fold the ironed edge to the back of the quilt and slip stitch it to the backing fabric over the stitching line.*

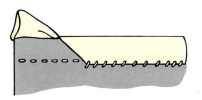

Turning the corner with French binding If the binding is very pliable, turn the corner and allow a natural mitre to form at the corner. The diagonal fold of this mitre can be secured with slip stitches.

Alternatively, bind the two opposite sides of the quilt first. Then bind the other two sides, catching in the binding on the first two sides to form a square corner, almost like a log cabin layout.

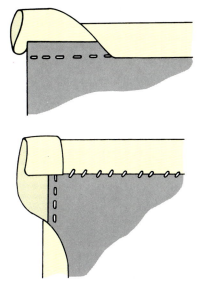

If the quilt sides are straight but the corners are curved, piece a *bias strip* onto the straight binding so that the binding can follow the curve.

Clip the curve before rolling the bias over and slip stitching it to the back of the quilt.

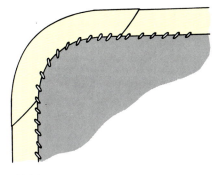

Self binding
If you want to bring the backing fabric over to the front to make a self binding, make sure you have about 5-10 cm (2-4 in) extra backing fabric.

For a rounded profile, cut the wadding the same size as the backing. Fold the wadding allowance in half, fold under a small seam allowance on the backing fabric and bring it over the raw edges to cover the wadding.

Another option is to cut the wadding the size of the finished quilt and to bring the backing over the raw edges to the front to meet the quilt top. Blind hem the rolled edge in place.

The backing fabric must be compatible with the quilt top if this method is used. Alternatively, the opposite procedure can be used by rolling the quilt top fabric to the back of the quilt to form a binding. With self binding the corners can be mitred or squared.

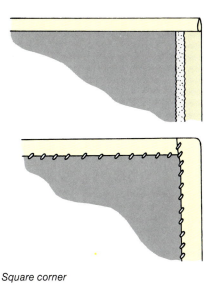

Square corner

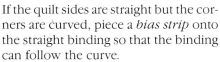

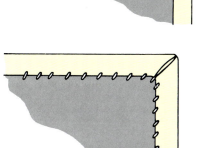

Once the quilt has been hemmed, the edges can be outline quilted about 3 mm (⅛ in) from the hem.

Folded edges *(Slip hemmed edges)*
This method does not require additional fabric and is suitable for reversible quilts. The quilting design must stop about 1.5 cm (⅝ in) from the edge so that the fabric is free to be folded over the wadding.

Trim the wadding to the exact quilt size. Now fold the excess fabric of the quilt top over the wadding and fold the excess backing inwards to align with the upper folded edge.

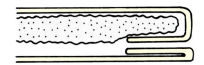

Slip hem the two edges together or make small running stitches through all the layers to give a quilted effect. For added strength, a second lane of quilting stitches can be made about 3 mm (⅛ in) from the folded edge.

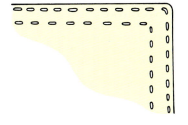

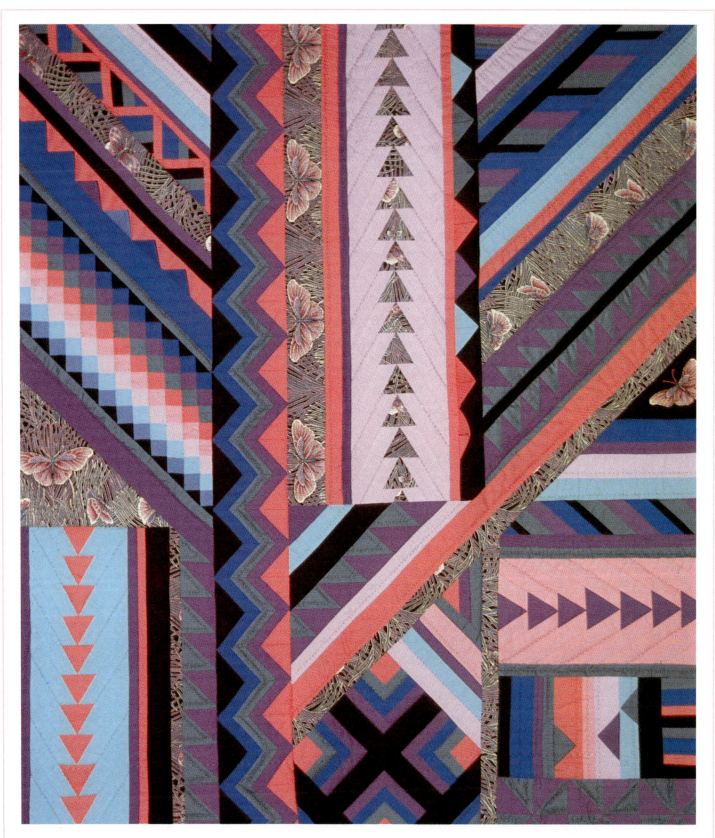

ABOVE
Quilt artist: **Margaret le Roux**
Barbara's Butterflies is a brilliant composition created by balancing strong diagonals with horizontals and verticals. Many different block designs with a strong Amish influence can be seen in this quilt. Excitement is added by the introduction of the floral butterfly fabric. Notice the prairie points.

OPPOSITE
Quilt artist: **Marietté Botha**
Prairie points make an attractive edging to this calico quilt.

AN EXTRA DIMENSION
Triangles made from squares is an exciting extension idea which gives a three-dimensional quality to basically two-dimensional patchwork. Wonderful illusions of space can be achieved by changing colours and using thin or transparent fabric.

1. *Cut a square of fabric, fold it in half and then fold the top corners to the centre to form a mitred triangle. Press the shape.*

2. *Work from the top edge and build horizontal rows of triangles onto a matching foundation fabric. Secure each triangle at the corners with four small stitches. The triangles can show the fold or face the other way, depending on the effect required.*

Folded squares can also make an outstanding Prairie point border.

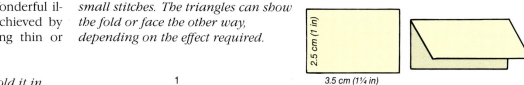

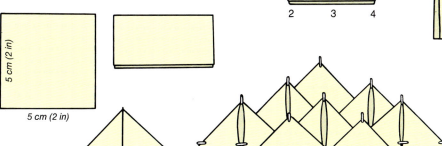

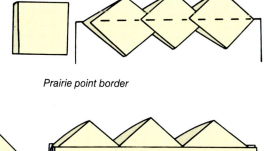

Prairie point border

PHILIP'S RADIANT NINE-PATCH QUILT

This single-bed quilt was made under the careful guidance and tuition of Pat Parker and Jenny Williamson who based their teaching on an original design by Blanche Young.

Step-by-step instructions are given to make this quilt using the quick cutting and piecing method described on page 46.

Study the section on the basic nine-patch described on page 48 and make a couple of blocks to ensure that you understand the technique. This basic design can easily be enlarged to make a double-bed quilt.

BASIC LAYOUT
200 x 161 cm (80 x 64 in) when finished
19 x 15 basic nine-patch blocks, each about 10 cm (4 in) square
285 blocks in total

REQUIREMENTS
Fabrics
Borders: 1.25 m (1.5 yd) of sprigged apple-green fabric for first border and 1.5 m (1.75 yds) of sprigged rust fabric for second border.
Lining: about 5 m (5.5 yd) or a 200 x 161 cm (80 x 64 in) cotton sheet.
Wadding: about 200 x 161 cm (80 x 64 in) polyester wadding.
Blocks: about 60 (not less than 48) different fabrics in light, medium and dark shades of two colour families (rust and blue). Choose pure cotton fabrics of the same type. You will need about 30 pieces of each family. Don't use plain fabrics or those with geometric designs.

The strips for this quilt are cut from about 120 x 25 cm (47 x 10 in) pieces of fabric, so buy pieces measuring 0.25 m (1/3 yd) or cut your old scraps into strips measuring 120 x 25 cm (47 x 10 in). There will be some wastage and a few blocks left over, but you do need extra to allow for good radiation. (Left over blocks can be made into a cushion or used as borders on curtains or pelmets.)

Use light, medium and dark prints, and small, medium and large designs. Choose shades of blue that move into a blue/green range, and rust through to apricot and dark red/brown. Organize the fabrics in pairs within the same family but with sufficient contrast so that you can definitely tell which colour is the darker. An unexpected colour can be used to give the quilt that extra 'zing'. For this quilt it is apple green.

You will need at least half the blocks to be medium-coloured, with more dark blocks for the outer areas than light blocks as these are only used for the centre of the quilt.

Equipment for marking and cutting
Perspex ruler or a stiff 61 x 5 cm (24 x 2 in) cardboard template.
Soft pencil or chalk.
Rotary cutter and Teflon cutting board.

General equipment
Medium-coloured sewing-machine thread.
Pins.
Quilting thread.
Spray starch.
Masking tape or double-sided adhesive (mirror) tape to mark the 8 mm (1/3 in) seam allowance on the machine plate.

METHOD
1. *Following the instructions for the basic nine-patch on page 48, make all your A and B blocks in light, medium and dark colours, using toning pairs in the blue and rust families. Don't forget the slightly larger than usual seam allowance of 8 mm (1/3 in).*

2. *Press the seams towards the sections that have* two *dark squares.*

TO ARRANGE THE BLOCKS
3. *Arrange the blocks on a large sheet, as Pat and Jenny suggested, so that the design can be picked up and held vertically to see if the design does radiate from light to dark. Start working from the centre with a group of light-coloured blocks and be sure to alternate the A and B blocks.*

4. Then add the medium and finally the darkest blocks on the outer edges.

5. Examine your quilt from a distance to see if you are happy with the design. (Try using a pair of binoculars, looking through them the wrong way round.)

6. Number the blocks across and down so that you cannot possibly make a mistake once you start joining all the blocks in their rows. Unpin the blocks from the background sheet and stack them in rows from the bottom of the quilt upwards.

TO JOIN THE BLOCKS

7. Join the first row (A) of blocks 1 to 15 across. Then the next row (B) from 1 to 15 across. Then join A to B, but make sure that you don't mix up the rows when joining row C.

8. Be careful not to lose the numbers on the blocks otherwise you could confuse the sequence. Continue joining the rows until the quilt top is assembled.

9. Press the seams in alternate directions. The quilt top will have 15 blocks across and 19 blocks down.

NOTE: The experienced quick quilter can join the blocks with chain stitching, in pairs, in a vertical arrangement until all the blocks from 1 to 15 are joined, without cutting the joining thread. Once all the piles are joined, join the rows.

ATTACHING THE BORDERS

10. Cut the apple-green fabric for the border 5 cm (2 in) wide, cutting two strips the length of the quilt plus twice the width of the green border (that is, an extra 5 cm (2 in) top and bottom for the mitre), and two strips the breadth of the quilt plus 5 cm (2 in) extra on each end.

11. Join the long strips to the quilt first and then the top and bottom, forming mitred corners (see page 60).

12. Cut the rust border 10 cm (4 in) wide, cutting two strips the length of the quilt plus 10 cm (4 in) extra at each end for the mitre, and two strips the breadth plus 10 cm (4 in) extra at each end for the mitre.

13. Attach the rust border in the same way as the apple-green border.

14. Prepare the textile sandwich of lining, wadding and nine-patch top for quilting. Quilt the blocks on the diagonal in one direction only.

15. Quilt the borders in the ditch (see page 31), using a quilting thread colour, such as ecru, that will create an interesting quilting design on the back of quilt and look good on all the different blocks.

16. Finish the quilt with a dark binding or roll the rust border over to the back to form a rolled edge about 5 cm (2 in) wide. For a larger quilt, add more borders.

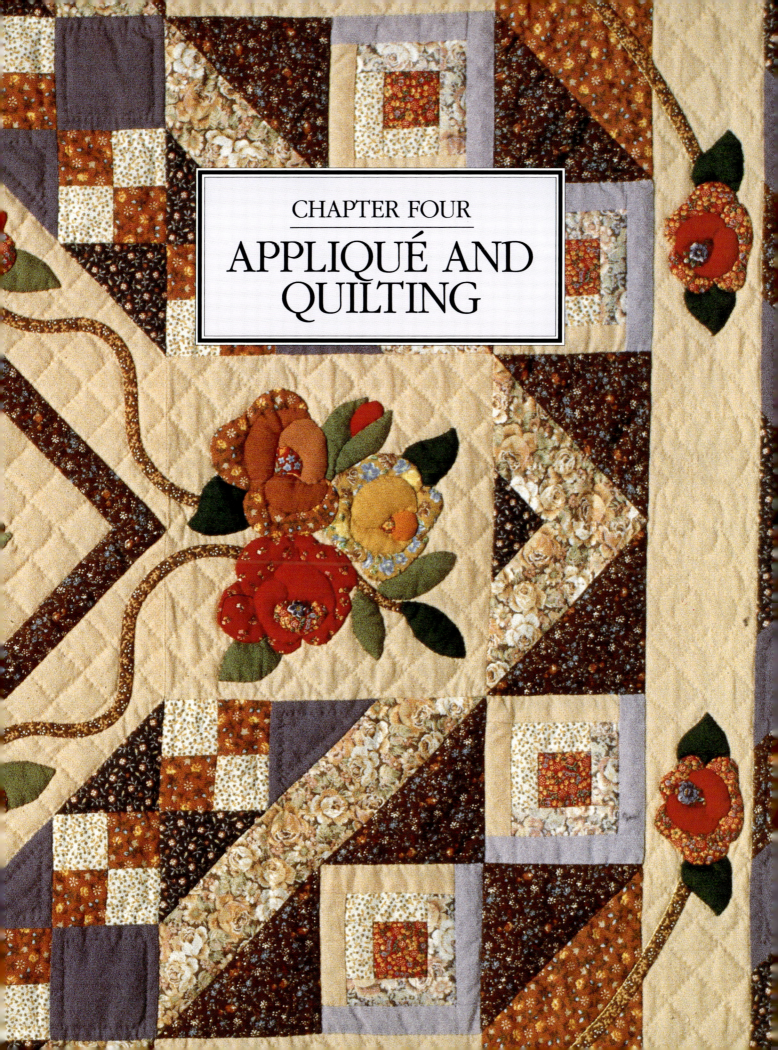

CHAPTER FOUR
APPLIQUÉ AND QUILTING

Appliqué is the name given to the technique of stitching fabric shapes and patches onto an existing or background fabric. This craft has quite practical origins, having been devised to repair worn or holed fabrics with patches. It became more decorative when the patches were cut into shapes and edged with fancy stitches.

Although appliqué is essentially a two-dimensional craft, the textures, stitches and shapes employed in a design provide a third dimension. Appliqué is often worked in conjunction with embroidery and quilting, the different craft-forms serving to complement and enhance one another.

The appliqué techniques described in this book have been kept as simple as possible, but some of the photographs illustrate the degree of complexity and intricacy which can be achieved once the basic elements of the craft have been mastered. How and where the appliqué will be used will determine the design and the colour, which in turn will influence the choice of thread and stitching technique.

GENERAL TECHNIQUES

SELECTING THE FABRICS

Fabric choice will depend on the amount of wear and tear and washing the quilt will have to stand up to. Your choice will be further influenced by whether the appliqué is to be hand or machine sewn. For hand appliqué, light- and medium-weight fabrics are recommended. Closely woven, natural fabrics such as lawn, chintz, gingham and lightweight wools are best as they are easy to fold. This is only a guide though, as any fabric can be used if the artist is experienced or particularly talented.

Machine appliqué allows a far larger fabric choice because no fold-over seam allowance is required, unlike the hand method which requires that seams be folded over and stitched, thus creating more bulk.

Fine fabrics like silk, dacron, tulle and lace as well as coarse, heavier fabrics, such as denim, corduroy, velvet, leather and suede can be used. However, when working with quilts, it is advisable to choose appliqué fabrics with the same weight and durability. It is wise to pre-shrink the fabrics and to check that they are colourfast before use.

PLANNING THE DESIGN

Colour choice is personal, but there are definite colour principles which you can employ when planning your designs (see Chapter 1, PATTERN AND COLOUR). All the colour principles described in that chapter apply to appliqué and piecing.

Pattern and texture The correct choice of pattern and the texture of the fabric is vital to the success of a design. For example, geometric fabrics create optical illusions, granny prints add charm, while textured fabrics give an added dimension.

ENLARGING THE DESIGN

Should you wish to enlarge your chosen design, first trace it onto a sheet of tracing paper. Place the tracing paper over some graph paper so that you have a squared-up drawing, or use a ruler and felt-tipped pen to make an evenly squared grid over the design (use the graph paper as a guide). Now, on a clean sheet of paper, draw another grid the size you require for the eventual design. The second grid must have the same number of squares as the original.

Copy the design square by square onto the larger grid, referring to the corresponding squares of the original grid. It may help to number the squares on both grids.

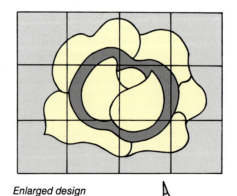
Enlarged design

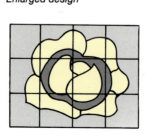
Original design

NOTE: *If the design is complicated, make a tracing from your enlarged design and, when assembling the appliquéd shapes onto the background, lay the tracing on top to ensure that all the pieces are correctly positioned. Should the design consist of many pieces, it may help to number the pieces on the drawing.*

TRANSFERRING THE DESIGN

There are several ways to transfer the designs to your background fabric:

Iron-on vilene is a transparent, bonded interfacing that is ideal for appliqué because it can be placed over the original drawing, and the shapes in the design traced onto it. These shapes are then cut out, ironed onto the wrong side of the fabric and used as a pattern for cutting out the fabric shapes.

The vilene backing strengthens the shapes and prevents fraying. Vilene is available in different thicknesses and should be chosen according to the fabric you are working with (single-layered appliqué shapes require a thicker vilene than multi-layered shapes).

Appliqué paper (bonding web) For simple appliqué shapes, the design is drawn onto the rough side of the paper and then cut out. This piece is then ironed, rough side down, onto the wrong side of the fabric to be used for the design. The fabric is cut around the appliqué paper and the paper peeled off the back, leaving an adhesive web of vilene. The appliqué piece is then placed in position on the fabric and ironed again. The design is now firmly fixed in place and can easily be machine stitched, using a closed zigzag.

Templates can be made if the design is simple or repetitive. Make the templates from cardboard or old X-ray plates, then place them directly on the fabric and cut around them.

Dressmaker's carbon and tracing wheel are also suitable. Place the carbon between the fabric and the design, and run the wheel along the design lines with enough pressure to transfer the design onto the fabric.

A second drawing (or cartoon as it is called in stained-glass appliqué) can be made and cut up into pieces. Place the pattern pieces on the right side of the fabric, draw around them and cut them out, leaving a 6 mm (¼ in) seam allowance where necessary.

A dressmaker's pencil or a very light pencil can be used to trace designs directly onto sheer (transparent) fabrics.

Freezer paper or plastic-backed brown paper This transfer method will be described below.

HAND APPLIQUÉ

BALTIMORE APPLIQUÉ AND QUILTING

I have chosen to describe the antique *Baltimore quilt* method of hand appliqué, as there is a wonderful revival in the making of these superb quilts, which were unique to the Baltimore quilters between 1845 and 1852. Only about 30 of these album quilts were made during that time, possibly executed by a number of different people, although signatures suggest that there might have been an original designer. The original Baltimore quilts were predominantly in a rich red and Victorian green on an off-white background. Yellow was used for highlighting and shaded blue fabric appeared frequently in the vases or the blooms. The main motifs used were baskets of flowers, wreaths, vases, posies and the cornucopia (Horn of Plenty). Fruit appeared with flowers, and in certain album quilts an important wedding document or bible was included.

The quilts were more elaborate in the centre and sometimes a snowflake block was included in the border (that is, a folded paper cut-out pattern [see illustration opposite] with the design cut from one piece of fabric).

REQUIREMENTS

Needles: sharp, fine crewel needles, No. 10 or No. 12.
Pins: fine, short pins are essential if you choose 'free-style' hand appliqué.
Scissors: fine, sharp embroidery scissors for cutting notches and clipping curves.
Marking pen or pencils.
Iron-on freezer paper (or plastic-backed brown paper).
Fabric: medium-weight 100% cotton in prints and plain colours.
Thread: colours to match the appliqué patches.

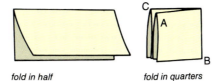
fold in half   *fold in quarters*

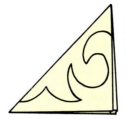
Fold A to meet B, then fold C backwards to meet B. Mark the design as shown and cut out through all the layers.

Methods of on-laid hand appliqué
There are different methods of stitching the appliqués onto the background:

Freezer paper Draw your design on the shiny side and cut out the design. Iron the freezer paper, shiny side down, onto the wrong side of your fabric. Cut out the design with a 4 mm (small ¼ in) turn-under seam allowance. Stitch the freezer paper-backed patch onto the background with an invisible hemming stitch (see illustrations on page 70).

Paper templates This method is the same as the traditional patchwork paper template method where the fabric seam allowance is folded over and tacked onto the paper. The tacked shapes are then placed on the background and hand hemmed in place.

Free-form appliqué (needle turn) Simply pin or tack the fabric shapes onto the background fabric, and appliqué by turning the edges under as you go. Use your needle or a toothpick to flick the seam allowance under. (Straight stitch the edges of problem fabrics first to prevent fraying. This line of stitching also provides a guide for folding under the seam allowance.)

Preparing the background
The basic design can be very lightly sketched onto the background but the top Baltimore-style quilters prefer not to mark the fabric and feel it is best to work with a top sketch as a placement guide. Alternatively, the sketch can be placed underneath the fabric and the design checked on a lightbox as you proceed.

Placement order
Work from the background forwards, that is, begin with the stems, then the leaves and finally the flowers. The edges of underlying leaves are not usually turned under as they will be hidden by the overlapping petals.

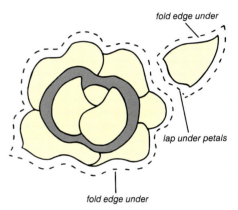
fold edge under / *lap under petals* / *fold edge under*

As the shapes are completed, the background fabric can be cut away from behind each appliqué as you work. If freezer paper or paper templates are used, the paper can be removed when the background fabric is cut away.

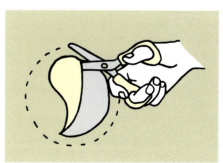

The appliqué stitch
Use a single strand of thread in a colour which matches the patch, not the background. The appliqué stitch is a small blind hem stitch. A tiny spot of thread shows at the front and a slightly longer thread is carried up the back.

Bring the needle through the background and catch a couple of threads of the fold of the appliqué. Re-insert the needle right next to the exit point into the background and move the needle about 3 mm (⅛ in) away to come up through the background and the appliqué again.

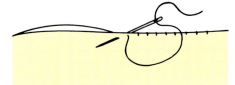

Another method is to slip the needle along the fold of the appliqué, pick up a few background threads and then re-insert the needle immediately into the folded edge.

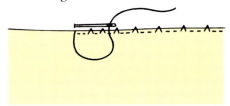

Tips for stitching
Curves Using very sharp scissors, clip notches into the convex curves about 3 mm (⅛ in) into the turn-under seam allowance.

Inner points (that is, concave curves) must be clipped to the turn-under line and a few extra stitches made at the point to hold the appliqué in place.

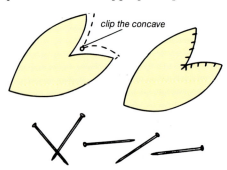

Corners Trim off the tip and turn the point down. Turn under one side and then the other. Stitch right to the point, make a few extra stitches and then stitch down the other side.

Circles To make perfect small circles, cut a thin cardboard template the size of the circle needed. Cut the fabric the size of the template plus 6 mm (¼ in) seam allowance. Run a gathering thread around the fabric shape, place the template on the wrong side of the fabric and pull up the gathers. Press the seam allowance around the circle, remove the cardboard and stitch the circle onto the background fabric.

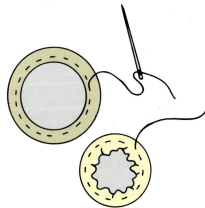

This method can also be used for padded circles: substitute wadding for the cardboard and blind hem the circle onto the background fabric.

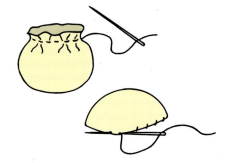

Stems Make a strip of bias binding (see page 74) the width of the stem plus seam allowance. Fold the bias in half lengthwise, wrong sides together and sew a narrow seam. Fold the seam allowance back under the bias and press. Stitch the concave (inside) curves of bias stems first, and then the outer curves.

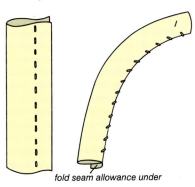
fold seam allowance under

Buds In-laid appliqué is often used for buds and the centres of flowers. Cut the bud fabric with a seam allowance. Make a small split in the green calyx and slip the bud shape into the green fabric. Turn under a small seam allowance on the green edge and blind hem the in-lay in place. This technique is the same as reverse appliqué (Mola).

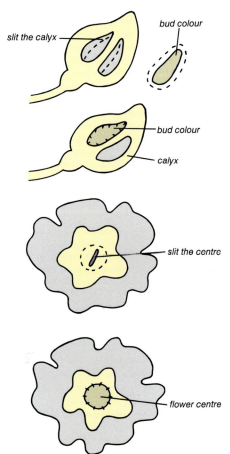

70

Extra dimensions
Bias binding flowers can be used to make zinnias, full-blown roses or chrysanthemums.

Follow the instructions for making bias binding on page 74, making the bias binding about 2.5 cm (1 in) wide and about 1 m (1 yd) long. Fold and iron the binding and then work running stitches in a zigzag along the length of the bias binding. Pull up to gather until you have a well-ruched strip. Begin the appliquéing of the bias in the centre and work outwards, underlapping the shapes as you proceed. Secure the bias with one stitch on each scallop.

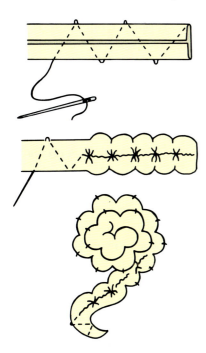

Quilt artist: **Janet Roche**
Work in progress. Detail showing ruched bias binding and a completed zinnia.

Three-dimensional rosebuds Make folded fabric rosebuds from a rectangle of fabric. Cut a rectangle about 12.5 cm x 7.5 cm (5 x 3 in) for large or medium buds and 7.5 cm x 5 cm (3 x 2 in) for small rosebuds.

1. *Fold over 2 cm (¾ in) to the wrong side along the long edge of the rectangle of fabric.*

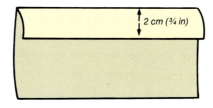

2. *Fold the left side down at right angles to the centre.*

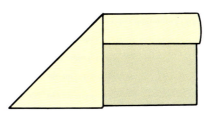

3. *Fold the right side so that it runs parallel to the diagonal left side, leaving a small space, about 6 mm (¼ in).*

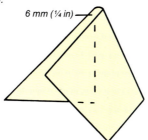

4. *Fold the left side from left to right at an angle, about 2 cm (¾ in) from the point.*

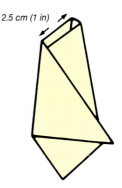

5. *Fold the right-hand side, from right to left at an angle, about 2 cm (¾ in) from the point and secure the cross-over with a pin or a stitch.*

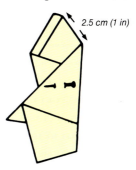

6. *Use your pattern as a guide and slip the folded bud under the calyx. Trim the base of the folded rose to fit neatly into the calyx.*

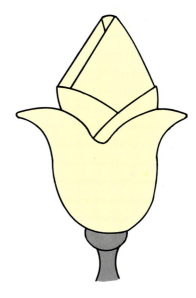

7. *Pin the folded edges in place and appliqué the calyx to the rosebud. Hem the outer edge of the rose to the background but leave the inner folds of the bud free.*

Embroidery details

In *traditional* Baltimore quilts certain decorative embroidery details were included, such as veins on leaves, petal divisions, stamens, insects and sometimes birds. However, there should not be more than 25% embroidery.

Buttonhole stitch can be used to appliqué motifs on Baltimore quilts, although it seems that on the traditional quilts buttonholing was used as an embellishment rather than just as a means of appliqué. Buttonhole stitch can be used on a folded edge (slightly open) or on a raw edge (very close).

I feel that in the revival of Baltimore-type quilts you can have a lot of fun using decorative stitches as your appliqué method (see Chapter Five for embroidery stitches).

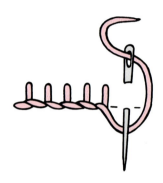

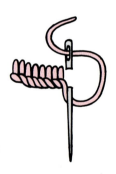

Quilting

The backgrounds of these album quilts vary a lot. The most common treatment is a single lane of echo quilting around the basic design, followed by cross-hatching as a filler. Other quilts have a mixture of echo quilting, the repetition of motifs that appear in the appliqué as well as feathers, wreaths, swags and filler quilting.

When choosing your background quilting design, make sure that it complements the design as a whole and that it can stand on its own as beautiful quilting, especially on the back of the quilt.

ABOVE
Quilt artist: **Marietjie Coertzen**
This prize-winning Baltimore sampler was hand appliquéd and hand quilted. Notice the different quilting designs, namely feathers and diagonal quilting.

TOP LEFT
Quilt artist: **Claire Grant**
The fabric shapes used for this holly wreath have been hand embroidered in place using decorative embroidery stitches instead of blind hemming.

TOP RIGHT
Quilt artist: **Claire Grant**
An example of Baltimore-style hand appliqué with embroidery details. The petals of the blue daisies have been worked in Portuguese border stitch (see page 94) and the stems in raised chain stitch.

LEFT
Quilt artist: **Marion Boltar**
(Loerie Quilters Guild)
Work in progress. This detail is from a panel of a friendship quilt entitled *Circles in the Forest*. The theme is re-inforced by the lanes of circular quilting.

BELOW
Quilt artist: **Lesley Campbell**
(Loerie Quilters Guild)
This detail from a friendship quilt shows the *Cockerel* panel which is hand appliqué, embellished with hand embroidery. The liberty print is the common denominator in each panel of this friendship quilt.

Quilt artist: **Lesley Turpin-Delport**
A beautiful example of shadow appliqué with embroidery details.

SHADOW APPLIQUÉ

Shadow appliqué is another hand-appliqué technique, using transparent fabric to create a very subtle and delicate effect which gives a gentle diffusion to the basic appliqué shapes.

METHOD

1. Transfer the design onto iron-on vilene, cut out the shapes and iron them onto your choice of fabric. Cut out the shapes without adding any fabric turn-under seam allowance.

2. Assemble the design directly onto the background fabric using a commercial glue stick or by using appliqué paper and ironing the shapes directly onto the background.

3. Cut a piece of sheer fabric the same size as the background fabric. Position it over the prepared appliqué and tack the layers together on the diagonals.

4. Using two strands of embroidery thread slightly darker than the appliqué fabric, make tiny running stitches through the background and sheer fabric layers, just outside the edges of the appliqué pieces. Add embroidery details once all the outlining is complete. Alternatively, quilt and appliqué at the same time (see steps 5 and 6).

5. For quilting, cut wadding and lining the same size as the background fabric, and sandwich the wadding between the lining and the completed shadow appliqué top.

6. Quilt around each appliqué shape using tiny running stitches. The design will have a shadowy effect as well as a plumpness created by the textile sandwich.

The background can have other quilting designs worked into it if necessary.

STAINED-GLASS APPLIQUÉ AND QUILTING

Stained-glass quilts simulate in fabric and bias binding the opalescence a real window achieves with coloured glass and lead cames. Choice of fabric is very important because the fabric shades give an illusion of illumination. Streaked, rippled, veined, bubbled and flecked fabric will all give an exciting opalescent effect. Batiked, hand-dyed and hand-painted fabric will also create an illusion of glass. The colours should be rich and jewel-like.

The black bias represents the lead cames and accommodates the curves around the appliqué shapes.

Do not use bought bias binding; make your own.

How to make bias binding
There are two different methods of making bias binding.

METHOD 1

1. Cut a square of fabric (that is, measure selvage to selvage and mark your square from that measurement).

2. Fold the square in half on the diagonal.

3. Use the fold line as your guide and mark parallel lines the desired width apart. For stained-glass appliqué, about 2 cm (¾ in) is ideal.

4. Cut out the strips.

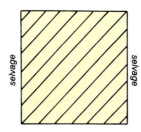

METHOD 2

1. Fold the square in half on the diagonal and cut along this line.

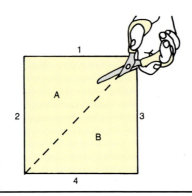

2. Re-position the triangles to form a parallelogram and sew the seam by machine.

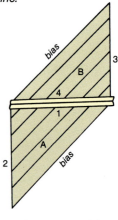

3. Iron the seam open and flat and draw lines of the desired width parallel to the diagonal (bias) edge.

4. Join the edges to form a tube, skipping one strip at the top. Sew this tube by machine.

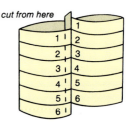

5. Cut along the drawn lines to form a continuous piece of bias binding.

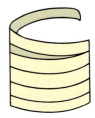

Quilt artist: **Annamarie Storm**
Superb illumination is achieved through the clever choice of fabric in this stained-glass rose design.

Stained-glass technique

1. *Make a full-size pattern of your design on paper and outline it in dark felt-tipped pen (this is called the cartoon).*

2. *Choose a colour that will appear frequently in the design as your background fabric.*

3. *Transfer the design onto your fabric with a pencil. If you cannot see through the fabric, use a lightbox or dressmaker's carbon. I have chosen my dining-room window as an example for the cartoon.*

4. *Make patterns for the coloured areas by tracing each shape onto tracing paper. Take each pattern piece to the centre of the lead came (that is, halfway under the bias binding).*

5. *Number or identify each colour on the cartoon and the tracing – not on your fabric.*

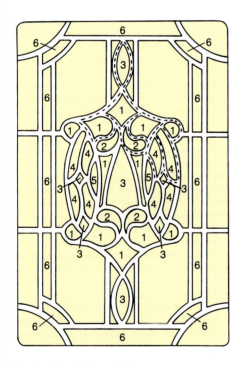

Key to stained glass window

1 – Orange   4 – Green
2 – Blue   5 – Dark green
3 – Lilac/Pink   6 – Yellow

6. *Cut out the coloured fabric shapes the exact size of the tracing. The colours will butt against each other and the edges will be covered by the bias binding.*

7. *Position the coloured shapes on the background fabric and tack the pieces in place, about 6 mm (¼ in) from the raw edge.*

8. *Prepare your black bias binding (see page 74) to a width of 2 cm (¾ in), marking the seam allowance on the black fabric with a white or silver pencil or a sliver of soap.*

9. *Turn under a 6 mm (¼ in) seam allowance on one side and press. Fold over the other side just under 6 mm (¼ in) to overlap the first, so that the bias is about 6 mm (¼ in) wide. Tack down the centre of the bias as shown.*

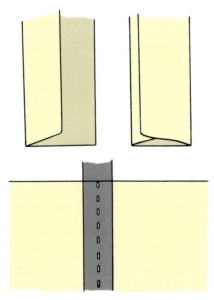

10. *Place the bias binding directly over the butting, raw edges of the coloured fabric (exactly like the lead in the original window design). The raw edges must be midway underneath the bias. When two lead lines meet, overlap one piece of bias with the other. Work out your bias placement so that you have as few cuts as possible.*

11. *To sew bias on curves, the inside (concave) edge of the curve must be pinned and sewn first and then the outside (convex) edge. The bias stretches to accommodate the outer curve.*

Sew on the bias binding with black thread using an invisible hem stitch, such as the Baltimore hem stitch on page 70.

Sew on small areas of bias at a time, pinning as you go.

Quilting the stained-glass appliqué

Stained-glass quilts usually have black lining fabric which allows a border to be folded over to finish the project (see page 61). Prepare the textile sandwich (see page 26) and quilt close to the bias with black thread. Bias that has been appliquéd directly to the background must be quilted on both sides. The coloured areas can be quilted on both sides of the bias (see fig. 1) or on the background side of the bias only (see fig. 2). Quilting on both sides of the bias will give the quilt a puffy appearance and a more attractive lining.

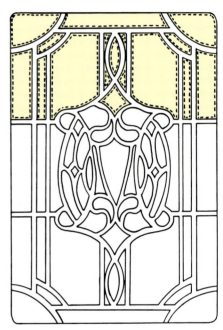

Fig. 1

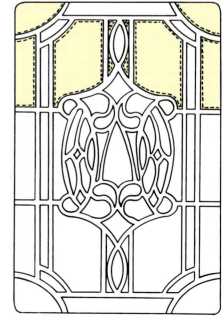

Fig. 2

RIGHT
Quilt artist: **The Loerie Quilters Guild**
This panel was inspired by a view in Sedgefield, Cape Province, South Africa, of a winding road, the estuary, distant mountains and the sunset sky. The choice of colours gives a luminosity which is so important in the stained-glass quilt technique.

BELOW
The stained-glass window in the author's dining room which inspired the quilt design described opposite.

REVERSE APPLIQUÉ *(Mola)*

Mola means cloth in the Tule dialect spoken on the San Blas Islands. This difficult technique of cutaway appliqué embroidery originated from the Cuna Indians of Panama and Columbia, but it has been adopted by the Western world. Two or three layers of coloured fabric are tacked together, then shapes are cut away and stitched to reveal the colour beneath. Traditionally, black or wine red appears on top, with acid green, orange, bright red, yellow or turquoise used underneath. It is essential to plan the design carefully.

Cut one large shape out of the first layer of fabric using fine embroidery scissors. Turn the edges under and sew them down with tiny, invisible hem stitches. Within the first shape cut another shape out of the second layer and finish the edges. Continue working this way until the entire design has been completed.

Decorative embroidery stitches can also be used in combination with reverse appliqué.

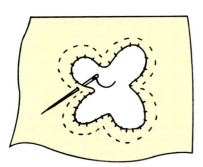

TOP RIGHT
Quilt artist: **Marie Peacey**
Mola at its best. This bird's head is part of an exquisite jacket.

RIGHT
Quilt artist: **Hennie Delport**
Reverse appliqué in striking colours of tan, black and white.

Marie Peacey is an expert on Mola, having worked with Cuna Indians of the San Blas Islands in Central America. She has developed her own unique style of Mola with cutaway work, painted fabric and embroidery. The Aztec-inspired panel featured here forms part of a large wall quilt.

FABRIC COLLAGE OR FREE-STYLE APPLIQUÉ

A more informal approach to appliqué quilts is to work directly onto the fabric, forming random shapes and building up the composition as you go along. Texture and stitching (hand or machine embroidery and quilting) can be used to give continuity and balance. This type of design is not pre-planned as pieces are attached and worked in as the design develops. As the name implies, free-style allows the creative appliqué artist freedom of choice when it comes to texture, colour and technique. Raw edges can be left and third dimensions introduced in the form of mixed media and found objects. Embroidery in fine detail is often used as a method of appliqué.

Batik, stencilling and silk paint allow the designers the freedom to colour their own fabrics.

Gauze bandage, rich velvets and smocked organza show the diversity of free-style fabric choice.

Always bear in mind that the basic principles of colour, composition and balance still apply if you want to create a successful wall quilt.

LEFT
Quilt artist: **Celia de Villiers**
'How cool and safe this cave . . . this place so elevated. Beyond lies the day, alive with life and rainbows . . . Dare we venture out and forsake this place of safety? We scurry, and peck and scratch and seek . . . ever watchful for the barrel of some killer's gun. Around us, the ghosts of our kin. Oh, my friends . . . they say we taste sweet to man's tongue. But what of us? Will they destroy us too . . . along with others of our kind?'

FIONA OGILVY

The above verse was written by Fiona Ogilvy especially for this wall hanging. This detail shows appliquéd guinea fowl standing in a cave surrounded by rich fabrics. A feeling of depth is created by the appliquéd flock of birds and lush plants.

BELOW LEFT
Quilt artist: **Celia de Villiers**
This quilt, entitled *Bouquet* contains no machine sewing. Appliqué, shadow appliqué, reverse appliqué, airbrushing, piecing and embroidery combine with hand-painted areas and a variety of fabrics to create this quilt of roses and ribbons.

OPPOSITE
Quilt artist: **Celia de Villiers**
This ethereal quilt entitled *Karoo* commemorates a family reunion in the spring of 1986. It had rained after eight years of drought and the desert was ablaze with colour. To re-create the textures and colours, Celia used miniature puff balls, strip-pieced hexagons and floral fabrics. Feather stitch, candlewicking and beading were used to blend the flowers with the background, while airbrush techniques add depth to the embroidery. Bourette and pongee silks, loom-state linen (unbleached 100% pure cotton) and jacquard cottons were used to add interest to the rather plain background.

OPPOSITE
Quilt artist: **Celia de Villiers**
'Lightning tears at the sky, and bolts of light reveal the secrets of this lush and vibrant place. The tiger's gleaming eye, the sheen of snakeskin, one bright feather and a myriad of rainbow petals . . . Only the adventurous answer the call of the jungle.'

FIONA OGILVY

This verse was written by Fiona Ogilvy to describe this quilt. The style of the quilt is almost a collage made up of hexagons stitched on top of each other. Sometimes they look like roses, and sometimes like peacock feathers. In *Midnight Jungle*, hand-dyed fabics, antique lamé lace and embroidered brocade contrast with the metallic tiger print and African fabric with leaf motif.

ABOVE
Quilt artist: **Celia de Villiers**
The detail of this hand-pieced and hand-quilted *Stars for Africa* quilt shows how Celia has depicted in star shapes the mineral riches of Africa (coal, diamonds, gold and copper); the colour of Mesembryanthemums (*vygies*) in the spring, and the aloe. Traditional shapes create a striking modern masterpiece quilt.

MACHINE APPLIQUÉ

Machine appliqué is stronger and faster than hand appliqué. The raw edges around the cut-out shapes are not folded over and tacked, but are covered with close zigzag stitch. A close zigzag setting creates a definite, ridged satin stitch, while a slightly open setting creates a more zigzag-like pattern. A fairly narrow stitch-width setting (about 2 on most machines) combined with a close zigzag setting (about ½) is suitable for most work. Bobbin tension can be made a little tighter than usual, as this will pull the top threads through to give a well-rounded satin stitch. Good quality thread will give a smooth satiny finish.

The colour of the thread used will depend on whether the design requires delineation, in which case a contrasting thread is preferable, or whether the colour zones are sufficiently marked, in which case a matching thread is best.

DIRECT APPLIQUÉ

This method is suitable for designs that are neither too large nor too complex. Prepare the shapes by using the following iron-on vilene technique:

1. Place the vilene, shiny side up, over the design and trace each shape separately using a soft pencil. Draw all details on each shape.

2. Where two raw edges meet, an underlap seam allowance of 6 mm (¼ in) must be marked on one piece of the vilene. This will be tucked under the adjacent piece when assembled. An underlap seam allowance is only added to a piece that will not change the design when the shapes are assembled. Superimposed pieces do not require an underlap seam allowance.

3. Cut out the pieces along the marked outlines. Iron the vilene shapes, shiny side down, onto the wrong side of the fabric. Remember the straight grain of the appliqué shapes must run in the same direction as the straight grain of the background fabric to prevent puckering and stretching.

4. Cut out the fabric shapes following the vilene outlines (no seam allowance is necessary).

5. Place the shapes directly onto the background fabric and tack in position. Use machine thread and tack as close as possible to the edge of the design so that the zigzag stitch will cover the tacking. A glue stick can be used to secure small pieces before machine stitching.

NOTE: Appliqué paper is also suitable for direct appliqué and eliminates the tacking or glueing step.

6. To secure the thread before zigzagging, set the machine on straight stitch, with the width on (0) and the length on (0) and make a few stitches – this knots the threads together. (End your work in the same way.) Now change the stitch width to 2 and the zigzag to ½ and machine stitch, working from the centre of the design outwards. Ensure that the needle is very sharp, and check that it enters the fabric from the raw edge inwards.

7. At a corner, leave the needle in the fabric on the outside of the line of stitches, lift the foot, turn the fabric and continue stitching so that the next stitch overlaps the previous stitch.

DOUBLE VILENE TECHNIQUE

This technique is suitable for designs that are too large for the entire design to pass comfortably through the machine. Instead small components are satin stitched and then attached either by hand or machine.

This technique allows you to embroider smaller shapes before attaching them to the background fabric. A slightly raised effect is an interesting feature of this technique.

1. Proceed as for direct appliqué from steps 1 to 5.

2. Now the second piece of vilene is used, hence the name 'double vilene technique'. Assemble the shapes according to your design on another piece of iron-on or ordinary vilene. The vilene must be large enough to protrude all round the edges of the design. Superimpose and underlap shapes where necessary. Tack or glue the pieces in position. If iron-on vilene is used, tack or glue the pieces on the dull *side.*

3. Place the design in the machine and satin stitch all the raw edges.

4. Carefully cut away the excess vilene without cutting into the zigzag stitching. Embellish the design as required with embroidery, beading or decorative stitching.

5. Assemble the design on the background fabric and sew it on by hand, using thread of the same colour and a small blind hem stitch over the satin-stitched edge. It can also be secured by machine by working an open zigzag over the satin-stitched edge. A straight stitch just inside the overlocked edge is also suitable.

DOUBLE FABRIC APPLIQUÉ

This is an extension of the double vilene technique and is used when three-dimensional shapes or reversible free-form images are required.

1. Proceed as for direct appliqué from steps 1 to 5.

2. Now assemble the fabric shapes on the wrong side of a second piece of fabric. The fabric must be large enough to protrude all around the edges of the design. Superimpose and underlap shapes where necessary. Tack or glue the pieces in position.

3. Place the shapes in the machine and satin stitch all the raw edges. Carefully cut away the excess fabric and add embroidery, beading or decorative stitching as required.

4. Proceed as directed in step 5 above.

QUILTING MACHINE APPLIQUÉ

Appliqué blocks can be joined together with or without sashing and then machine quilted in the ditch to hold the wadding and lining together. Some other designs lend themselves to echo quilting by machine or by hand to accentuate the image and create a rhythm.

The double vilene appliqué is complemented by a machine-quilted background of cross-hatched diamonds.

The use of a twin needle gives a very subtle quilted effect. This needle fits on most machines, and in combination with different settings and cams is excellent for creating many different images.

ABOVE
Quilt artist: **Adrienne Yates**
A delightful wall quilt combining machine appliqué, cathedral window patchwork and hand-embroidered details. Notice how the trapunto quilting gives extra 'plumpness' to the ladies of *The Quilting Party*.

RIGHT
Quilt artist: **Glenda Kaplan**
Corded hair and soft sculpturing of the faces and hands give a three-dimensional quality to this wall hanging.

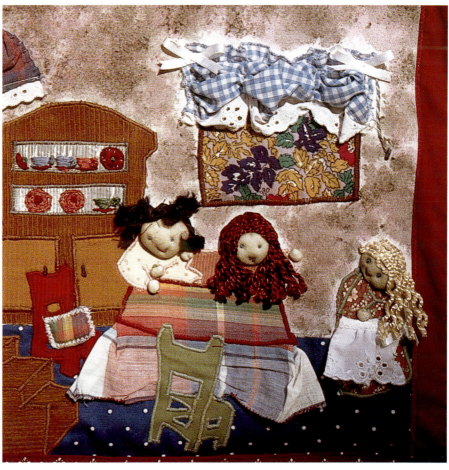

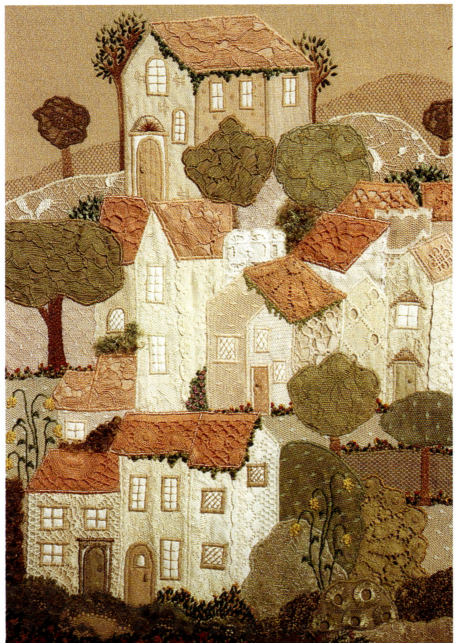

OPPOSITE
Quilt artist: **Edelgard Katz (Weiner Studio)**
Inspired by a greetings card, this village was machine appliquéd in plain and printed fabrics and decorated with embroidery details. A change in scale creates a feeling of depth.

ABOVE LEFT
Quilt artist: **Adrienne Yates**
A stay in Denver, Colorado inspired the creation of this appliqué entitled *The Picnic*. Notice the twin needle quilting on the picnic rug and how the use of spider's web, chain stitch, buttonhole stitch, bullion knots, French knots and satin stitch gives added dimension to the flower beds.

LEFT
Quilt artist: **Denise Schlesinger (Edelmuth Studio)**
Basic appliqué overlaid with tulle and lace add texture and interest to this village scene.

APPLIQUÉ BOUQUET QUILT

Step-by-step instructions are given for making this beautiful appliqué quilt from start to finish.

Machine appliqué, with hand embroidery for finishing touches, makes this quilt a fairly quick project, especially if you use pre-quilted seedcloth (unbleached 100% pure cotton) for the background. This quilt can be made to fit a king-size, queen-size or a double bed by trimming the borders to suit the size of your bed.

REQUIREMENTS

6 m (6.5 yd) by 150 cm (60 in) wide pre-quilted ecru cotton fabric for the background.
25 cm (10 in) each of a selection of pure cotton fabrics in shades of pink, blue, mauve, apricot and yellow for the flowers, and green for the leaves.
A selection of embroidery thread in matching shades.
Sewing machine thread in matching shades.
About 2 m (2 yd) of iron-on vilene
20 m (about 22 yd) of apricot bias binding for the bow.
About 9 m (about 10 yd) of light and dark green bias binding for the stems.

METHOD

1. Enlarge the bouquet design on page 108 and be sure to reverse the design for opposite corners.

2. Make four sets of appliqué flowers using the double vilene technique.

3. Embroider the centres of the flowers in French or bullion knots (see page 92 and 93), using two or three strands of embroidery thread in shades to suit your fabric. Work the stamens in extended French knots or extended fly stitch.

4. Now prepare the pre-quilted background fabric: cut the 6 m (6½ yd) length in half to make two 3 m (3¼ yd) lengths. Take one of these lengths and cut it in half lengthwise to make two long border strips. Put these border strips aside.

5. To assemble the appliqué flowers on the centre panel, first make a tracing of the bouquet design so that you have a top reference.

6. Spread the background fabric on your bed and position the appliquéd flowers in the bouquet design, with one pair placed on the bottom corners and the other pair, facing inwards, on the pillow area.

7. Arrange the light and dark green bias binding stems directly on the background, pinning and tacking as you go. The bias binding must be folded in half and only stitched on one side. Tuck the raw ends under the flowers or satin stitch the ends to neaten.

8. Hand or machine stitch the appliquéd flowers plus the bias stems to the background. Use matching thread on top and ecru for the bobbin to give a reversible quilt. Make the bow from apricot bias binding: fold it in half lengthwise and straight stitch or hand hem it in position.

9. Use the ruched bias binding method described on page 71 to make the centre of the bow.

10. Once all the appliqués have been completed, join the side panels using a flat-fell seam, so that both sides are very neat.

11. Finish the quilt by attaching apricot bias binding onto a straight or scalloped edge.

NOTE: *To cut a scalloped edge, make a paper template of scallops using a side plate to work out the curves. Start in the centre of the border and work towards the corner, making sure that the scallops are equally distributed and that the corners are gently rounded.*

ABOVE
Quilt artist: **Rachelle Druian**
Showing the arrangement of the appliqué bouquets on the quilt.

OPPOSITE
Work in progress. Notice the bias binding stems and bow.

FLAT-FELL SEAM

1. With wrong sides together, position the two pieces of fabric so that the bottom piece protrudes as shown, and machine stitch.

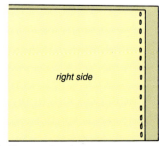

2. Turn under the edge of the wider seam allowance to make a narrow seam and tack flat, covering the raw edge of the under seam allowance. Press and machine stitch close to the edge. One side will show two rows of stitching, while the other side shows a joined seam and one line of top stitching.

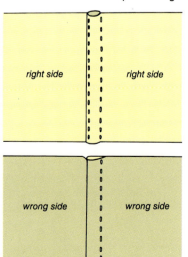

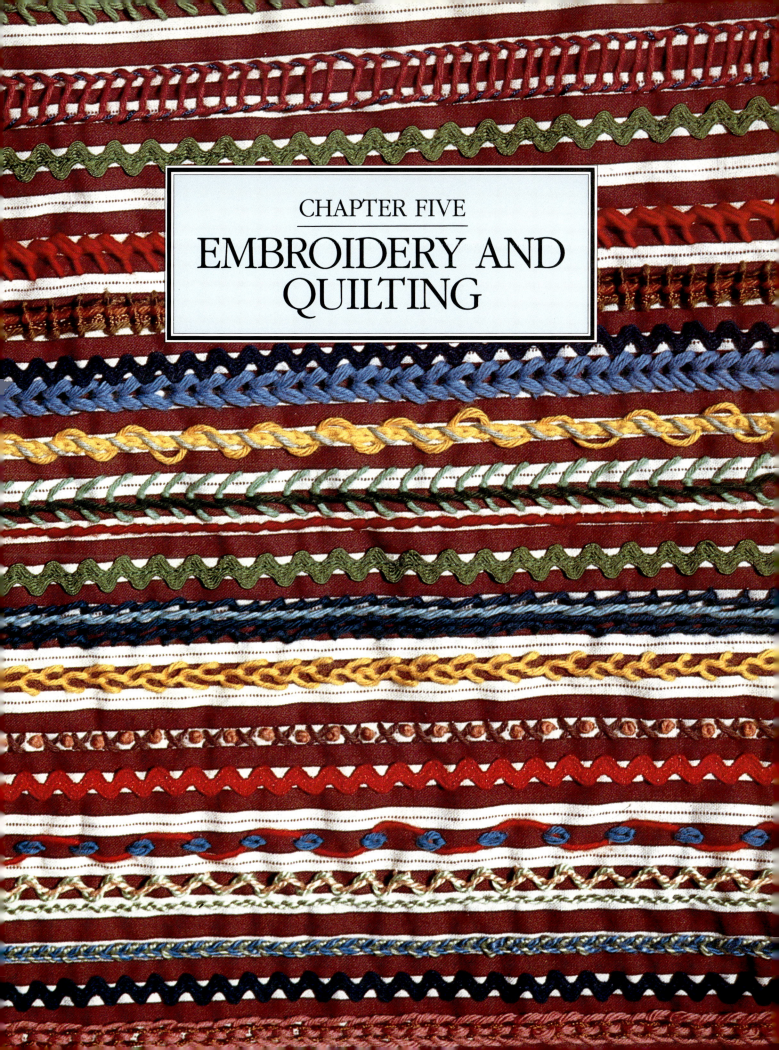

CHAPTER FIVE
EMBROIDERY AND QUILTING

A knowledge of basic embroidery stitches combined with a creative imagination provides the designer with a wonderful means of self-expression. Embroidery is like painting with thread and can provide the finishing touches on pieced or appliquéd quilts.

BASIC REQUIREMENTS

Before you begin, make sure that you have the following:
Needles: a good selection of very sharp to blunt-tipped needles (for wools or weaving) is essential.
Scissors: small, sharp pointed.
Thimble.
Thread: it is handy to have different types of embroidery thread. There is an excellent selection available, such as six-strand cotton, cotton perlé, crewel wool, metallic thread, crochet cotton and new textured wools.
Beeswax: to prevent knots and tangles
Embroidery hoop: to keep the ground fabric taut while the embroidery is being worked.
Fabrics: any fabric is suitable for decorative embroidery. The appliqué or pieced background will dictate your choice of thread and stitch technique.

TRANSFERRING THE DESIGN

There are a number of methods for transferring the design onto fabric:

Tracing paper

Use masking tape to attach your design to a window-pane. Place a piece of tracing paper over it and trace the outlines with a pencil.

Go over the design on the reverse side of the tracing paper, then place this side against your fabric and draw over it with enough pressure to transfer the design onto the fabric.

Hot transfer pencil

Trace the design onto tracing paper and go over the back of the design with a hot transfer pencil. Iron the design onto the background fabric.

Tracing directly from a drawing

This can be done if the fabric is transparent. Place the fabric over the design and trace over the outlines with a pencil. Use dressmaker's pencils in pink, blue or white or use a fabric pen which washes out or fades after 24 hours. A soft pencil (2B) is my personal choice.

Dressmaker's carbon

Trace the design onto tracing paper. Place the dressmaker's carbon face down between the background fabric and the tracing. Go over the outlines to transfer the design.

HAND EMBROIDERY

Most fine embroidery is worked using only two strands of six-strand embroidery thread. Bullion knots and French knots work well with three strands, while grub roses require three to six strands, depending on the size required. For bold effects, use many strands of embroidery thread or wool yarn, but do use thread that is compatible with your background fabric, that is silk on silk, cotton on cotton and so on.

Cut the threads about 50 cm (20 in) long and wax them if necessary to prevent tangles and knots. Begin with a back stitch and not a knot.

USEFUL EMBROIDERY STITCHES

The stitches illustrated below are the ones I find particularly useful. These stitches are then followed by a random selection of exciting composite stitches which are described in detail. Embroidery stitches can be used as an appliqué method and the purpose of the embroidery is both decorative and functional. Reverse appliqué (Mola work) also employs a lot of embroidery.

chain stitch

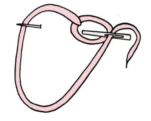

detached chain stitch (lazy daisy)

stem stitch

back stitch

buttonhole stitch

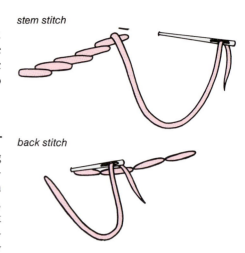

French knot

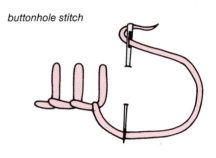

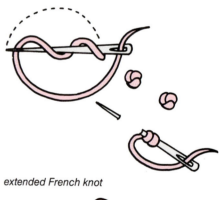

extended French knot

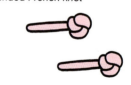

couching

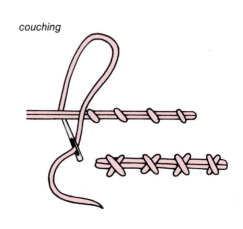

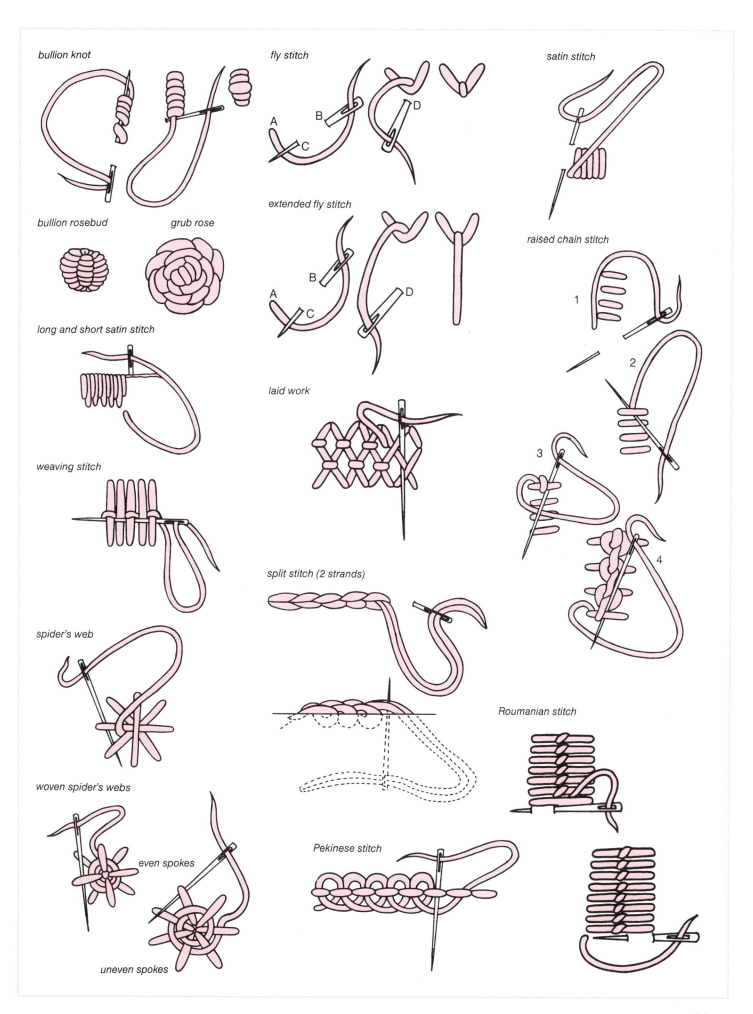

COMPOSITE EMBROIDERY STITCHES
Portuguese border stitch

Make a foundation row (ladder) of evenly spaced, straight stitches. Bring the needle through at the base of the ladder and work the right-hand side with the thread on the *left* of the needle. Carry it over and under the first two bars; and then over the same two bars and under the *second* bar only, without piercing the fabric. Continue to the top of the row. Now work the left-hand side in the same way with the working thread to the right of the needle. Do not pull the stitches too tightly.

Striped woven band

Make a foundation row (ladder) of evenly spaced, straight stitches. Thread two needles with different colours and, starting at the top, bring them through the fabric, side by side. Pass the light thread *under* the first bar and leave it lying. Then take the dark colour and pass it *over* the first bar and under the second bar and the light thread. Leave the dark thread and pass the light thread *over* the second bar and *under* the *third bar* and the dark thread. Continue in this manner to the end and begin each new row from the top.

Raised stem stitch

Make a foundation row (ladder) of evenly spaced straight stitches and work your stem stitch on the rungs only, without piercing the fabric. Always work in the same direction.

Quilt artist: **Madge Wulfsohn**
Work in progress. The wing of this barn owl has been embroidered in striped woven band stitch.

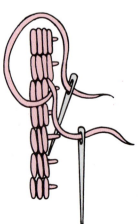

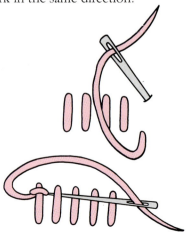

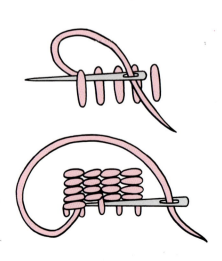

Whipped chain stitch
Make a foundation row of chain stitch. Using a contrasting thread, pass the thread over and under each link of the chain without penetrating the fabric.

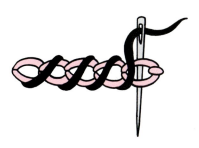

Turkey work
This is a divine stitch for a fluffy, three-dimensional effect. Bring the needle through the fabric from the front to the back *without a knot* and leave about 1 cm (½ in) of thread sticking out. Make a back stitch around the protruding tail (A) and let the needle exit right next to the original tail (B). Pull the thread firmly and make the back stitch securing the original tail (tuft). Work another back stitch, but this time leave a loop (C) and come up next to the previous back stitch.

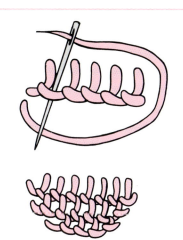

Semi-detached buttonhole stitch
This is almost like miniature crochet and is a superb stitch for three-dimensional leaves or wings.

Make a foundation row of buttonhole stitches with small spaces between each vertical spoke. Now turn the work around and work a buttonhole stitch into each of the horizontal loops of the original buttonhole without picking up the ground fabric. Do not pull the thread too tightly. Continue to the end of the foundation row. Turn your work around and buttonhole into the loops of the row you have just completed. At the end of a row you can secure the thread into the ground fabric or you can simply turn around and continue buttonholing into the last stitch.

The other side of the shape can also be worked in exactly the same way, laying down another foundation row of buttonhole into the gaps of the first foundation row. Taper the shapes by 'casting off' stitches: skip the first and last stitch in the row or increase the shapes by working into the same loop a couple of times.

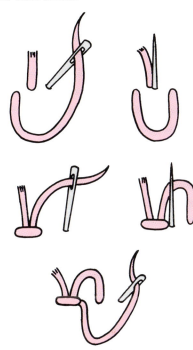

Alternate a loose loop stitch with a tight anchoring back stitch. At the end of a line, cut off the thread leaving approximately 1 cm (½ in) on the right side. Fill the area with individual lines of turkey work. Cut the loops and trim the tufts to fill the space. The loops can also be left untrimmed.

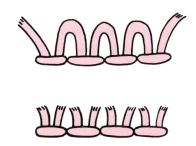

Quilt artist: **Madge Wulfsohn**
This brown hooded kingfisher is a fine example of how embroidery stitches can be used creatively.

STITCHES FOR FREE-STYLE FOLIAGE

Thorn stitch

This stitch resembles a thorny stem or a fern frond. Make a long straight stitch and catch the stem in place with a series of cross-stitches with the cross-over at the lower end. The spikes of the cross-stitch can increase in length down the original, long straight stitch.

Wheat ear stitch

This is another delightful foliage stitch. Make two straight stitches A and B. Bring the thread through the fabric a small distance below these two stitches at C and pass the needle under the two stitches without entering the fabric. Close the 'chain' at C and come out again at D to begin the 'ear' of wheat.

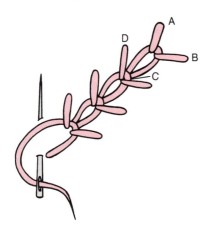

Lazy daisy filling stitch

Single daisy stitches set between two right-angled straight stitches make up this filling. The stitches in each row should be set alternately to those of the previous row to form diagonal lines across the filling.

Feather stitch

Work a single feather stitch. The base of the first stitch forms the branch of the second stitch. Work a stitch to the left on the same level and then to the right. Continue working these two movements alternately.

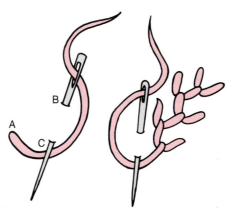

Looped bullion knot

To create a full-blown rose, make four bullion loops by working 20-twist bullion knots with the point of return as close as possible to the point of entry. Then work three to four loops in the space between the first four loops. The loops must look intertwined.

When you start playing with embroidery there are so many creative stitches that the combinations are limitless.

Choose your favourite stitches and combine them with appliqué, piecing and quilting.

ABOVE
Quilt artist: **Salli van Rensburg**
A twisted cable quilt design frames the embroidered posy panel. Notice the effective use of bullion knots.

OPPOSITE
Quilt artist: **Claire Grant**
Appliqué and embroidery combine to re-create a picture of a country house with its charming flower-filled garden.

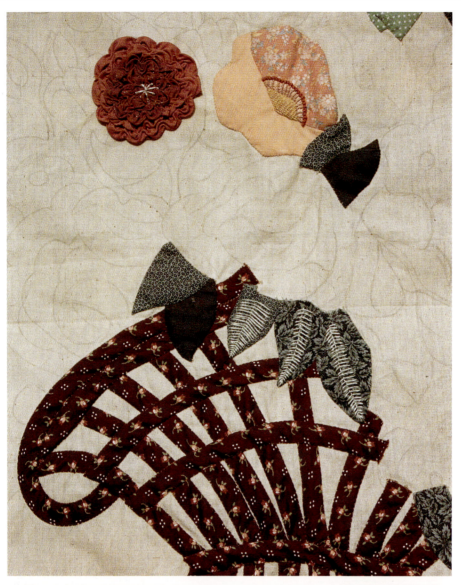

OPPOSITE
Quilt artist: **Claire Grant**
Hand appliqué attached with buttonhole stitch. The bee is a beautiful example of turkey work.

BELOW OPPOSITE
Quilt artist: **Denise Pearce**
Trapunto quilting gives added dimension to these embroidered flowers. The pink daisies are embroidered in woven back stitch and the basket in raised stem stitch.

LEFT
Quilt artist: **Janet Roche**
Work in progress showing a bias binding basket.

BELOW LEFT
Quilt artist: **Lesley Turpin-Delport**
Work in progress. Raw silk is hand appliquéd in place with colonial/French knots. The shapes are lightly stuffed before closing. Notice the Portuguese border stitch on the leaves.

BELOW
Quilt artist: **Blanche Sessel**
Perle embroidery thread instead of normal quilting thread has been used for the echo quilting to give a coarser effect.

OPPOSITE
Quilt artist: **Madge Wulfsohn**
Part of the magical garden growing out of a tulle underlay is visible in this detail of *Fantasy Castle*. Silk and organza blooms are attached with embroidery stitches, the contrast in the scale of the flowers being achieved by the use of different types of embroidery thread.

BELOW OPPOSITE
Quilt artist: **Ann Foulner**
Free-style embroidery using six-strand floss and four-strand cotton embroidery thread.

RIGHT
Quilt artist: **Adrienne Yates**
Detail of *The Picnic* showing the basic fabric which has been over-embroidered to give added dimension to the surface.

BELOW
Quilt artist: **Moira Ryder**
Detail of a crazy quilt. Each block has been hand pieced and hand embroidered in perle embroidery thread.

CANDLEWICK EMBROIDERY AND QUILTING

In the early American pioneering days, necessity became the mother of invention and beautiful embroidery was created by using the cotton wick for candles. Although other embroidery stitches were used (turkey work, satin stitch and stem stitch), traditional candlewicking was done with pure cotton thread worked in colonial knots, following the outline of a design. The background fabric was always pure cotton and the work was white on white or cream on cream. The antique candlewick work was not quilted.

Today candlewicking is done on natural or coloured fabric using the colonial knot or the French knot (one twist for fine detail or two twists for a bolder effect). Four-strand cotton thread is the best yarn to use.

Candlewicking is in fact an embroidery technique which, together with quilting, makes exciting designs and dimensions possible.

COLONIAL KNOT

Pull the thread through the fabric. Place the needle under the thread, sliding the needle from left to right (A). Wrap the thread over the top of the needle from right to left creating a figure eight (B). Insert the needle into the fabric close to where it emerged; pull the working thread taut with your left hand so that a firm, tight knot is formed (C). Pull the needle to the wrong side of the fabric thus forming a colonial knot. Let the needle emerge in the next dot.

NOTE: *If you are left-handed, reverse the procedure as shown.*

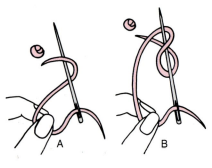

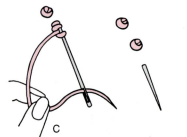

Colonial knot – right handed

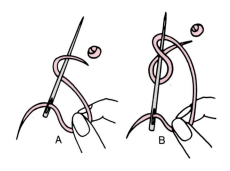

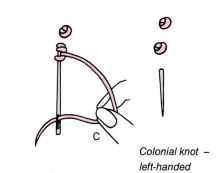

Colonial knot – left-handed

REQUIREMENTS
A pair of scissors.
A water-soluble pen or a soft pencil.
Embroidery needles (chenille needles are ideal).
An embroidery hoop.
Beeswax.
100% natural or coloured cotton fabric.
Candlewick yarn: No. 8 (fine) or No. 5 (coarse) candlewick yarn or 4 strands of embroidery cotton.

METHOD

1. *Place the fabric over the candlewick design. You should be able to see the dots through the fabric. If not, hold the fabric and the pattern up to the light or against a windowpane and lightly mark the design onto the right side of the fabric with a marking pen or soft pencil.*

2. *Insert the fabric into the embroidery hoop to hold the fabric taut.*

3. *Cut the yarn in 50 cm (20 in) lengths and run them lightly over the beeswax to hold the threads together. (This is not necessary if the thread is mercerized.)*

4. *If you wish to trapunto quilt (see page 26) the candlewicking, use a piece of muslin as a backing for the fabric. Once the embroidery is complete, the weave can be opened at the back of the design and padded with polyester wadding. Close the slit by pushing the weave together again. The background can also be quilted with echo quilting using the 'textile sandwich' which consists of top fabric, flat polyester wadding and lining (see page 26).*

5. *Work colonial or French knots on the dots and stem stitch or chain stitch along the lines. Work satin stitch or small French knots to fill in areas. Other embroidery stitches that I find complementary to candlewicking are whipped chain stitch and turkey work which gives a tufted effect (see pages 94 and 95 for embroidery stitches).*

6. *Remove the fabric from the hoop when all the stitching is complete. Rinse the fabric in cool water to remove the marks left by the marking pen. Now wash again in very hot water. This will shrink the fabric, holding the stitches firmly in place. Roll the fabric in a towel to remove the excess water, then allow to dry.*

7. *Iron the fabric gently on a padded surface with the design face down.*

Be adventurous and add coloured embroidery when candlewicking and quilting.

Quilt artist: Janet Roche
This quilt panel is in candlewicking, embroidery and trapunto. The heart shape is accentuated by the French knot violets.

Candlewicking the textile sandwich

Another method of candlewicking with quilting is to mark the design onto the top fabric and then to prepare the 'textile sandwich' (see page 26) before you begin candlewicking. The colonial knots are then made right through the three layers so that the embroidery and quilting is performed in the same operation. This method gives a lower profile than trapunto with echo quilting, but is much quicker.

Quilt-as-you-go candlewicking

Candlewicking and trapunto lend themselves to the 'quilt-as-you-go' technique.

Many quilters do not enjoy working with the bulk of a full-sized quilt. In the 'quilt-as-you-go' technique the large quilt is divided into more manageable units which are individually quilted. This type of quilt must be carefully planned and designed before the trapunto is done, otherwise the sashing or borders will not fit, as the trapunto diminishes the size of the original block.

Assembling the quilt

Once all the blocks have been quilted, the following different methods of assembly may be used.

1. The blocks may be joined directly in rows. Butt the blocks one against the other, stitching the top fabric together first, then the wadding, butting it together with herring bone stitch. Finally lay one side of the lining down flat and overlap with the other piece, turning under a small seam allowance. Blind hem the lining seam.

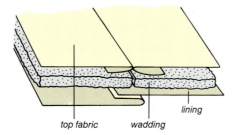

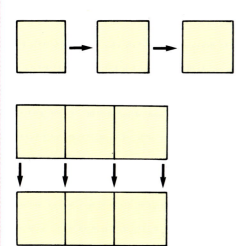

Joining rows of blocks

2. The 'quilt-as-you-go' blocks can also be joined with sashing which can be made from a sprigged fabric which complements the blocks. Lace-trimmed or hand-quilted sashing may also be used.

Some quilters prefer to assemble the quilted blocks and sashing before quilting the sashing. Transfer the quilting design onto the sashing and then assemble the blocks and sashing as shown below.

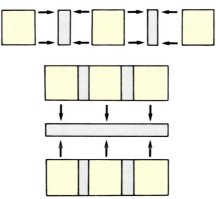

Joining blocks with sashing

Once the top of the quilt has been assembled, tack wadding to the back of the sashing. Now tack a complete lining to the quilt to provide a perfect back. Quilt the design on the sashing through the 'textile sandwich' and quilt in the ditch around each block.

3. The sashings can be quilted separately before joining them to the blocks. Add the sashing to the blocks by matching the top fabric of the quilted block to the sashing. Butt the wadding together and hand hem the lining, turning under a small seam allowance. The back of the quilt will be perfectly neat but not quite as reversible as the previous method (see Step 1 above). The seams on the back of the quilt can be covered with narrow lace strips, if desired.

4. It is also possible to use muslin as the backing when quilting the blocks and sashing. Add a lining to the quilt once you have finished quilting the blocks and sashings.

If this method is used, the layers can be tied or button quilted to prevent the lining from bagging. The border can also be rolled to the front for extra strength (see page 61).

Button quilting requires buttons to be placed at strategic points on the back of the quilt. Make a strong back stitch on the wrong side of the quilt, pushing the needle up at an intersecting point on the front so that the stitches will not show. Return to the underside and pick up the button. Pull the thread tight and push the needle through to the front again. Continue in this fashion until the button feels secure, then end with a couple of strong back stitches underneath the button.

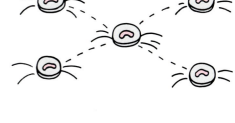

Tied quilting provides another method of sewing the three layers together. This method is only used if the wadding is too thick for conventional quilting. Use a chenille needle and wool or fancy embroidery thread and make one stitch through all the layers, leaving a long end on the top of the quilt. Make a back stitch and bring the needle up to the top again. Tie the ends together into a strong knot or bow.

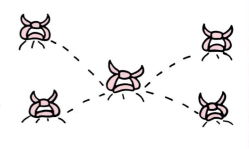

TRAPUNTO CANDLEWICK QUILT

Step-by-step instructions are given for making this candlewick embroidered Rose-Wreath Quilt from start to finish.

This quilt is entirely hand-made. Six rose-wreath panels are worked separately and then joined to the cross-hatched borders to make a 275 x 250 cm (108 x 100 in) quilt, suitable for a double or queen-size bed.

REQUIREMENTS
5.75 m (6⅓ yd) by 150 cm (60 in) wide seeded cotton for the top fabric.
4.5 m (5 yd) muslin for trapunto section.
5.75 m (6⅓ yd) seeded cotton for lining.
1 ball No. 5 candlewicking thread.
1 chenille needle for candlewicking.
1 reel of quilting thread for quilting, or No. 8 candlewicking thread for coarse quilting.
Dark pink and avocado-green embroidery thread for embroidery details.
Bundles of soft polyester wadding for trapunto quilting.
A large sheet of polyester wadding for background quilting. The amount will depend on the width available and the type of wadding you choose.
4B (soft) pencil for marking the design on the fabric.

METHOD

1. Cut out 6 squares each measuring 75 x 75 cm (29½ in x 29½ in) from top fabric, muslin, lining and flat wadding respectively.

2. Cut 2 strips, each measuring 275 x 52 cm (108 x 20½ in) of top fabric, lining and wadding for the side borders; another 150 x 52 cm (60 x 20½ in) strip from top fabric, lining and wadding for the bottom border; and one long strip of fabric measuring 250 x 12 cm (98½ x 4¾ in) for the top edge of the quilt.

3. Enlarge the rose-wreath design provided on page 122 and transfer the design onto the six panels using the layout on page 123 as your guide.

4. Mark a 1 cm (½ in) seam allowance around each square. Crease the panel on the diagonal and mark diagonal quilting lines 5 cm (2 in) apart. Then cross-hatch in the opposite direction to form diamonds.

5. Pin the six panels together to check that all the quilting lines match.

6. Mark a 1 cm (½ in) seam allowance on the border panels and line them up with the six-panel centre section. Transfer two of the four roses in the design onto the bottom edge of each of the long border strips and two to each end of the short bottom border strip. Once the quilt is complete and the borders mitred, the roses will join to complete the design of four roses.

7. Mark the diagonals and then cross-hatch the border panels, checking that the lines all match up and leaving a roll-over seam allowance of about 12 cm (4¾ in) for finishing the quilt.

8. Once you are sure that all the quilting lanes line up, begin working one rose-wreath panel at a time. Tack muslin to the back of the panel and work all the colonial knots on the rose outlines with ecru No. 5 candlewicking thread.

9. When all the ecru knots have been completed, embroider the rose centres

Quilt artist: **Lesley Turpin-Delport**
Work in progress. The centres of the roses are worked in dark pink colonial knots using four strands of embroidery thread.

in dark pink colonial knots using four strands of embroidery thread. Work the leaves in whipped back stitch, using the candlewicking thread for the back stitch and three strands of green thread for the whipping.

10. Once all the panels have been embroidered, trapunto quilt the roses and the leaves using the soft bundles of polyester wadding (see page 26).

11. Candlewick and embroider the roses on the border panels. (These roses are not trapunto quilted, although you can place a small piece of muslin behind the rose sections to allow the cavities to be filled.)

12. Now prepare all the panels and borders for the cross-hatch quilting, using the textile sandwich technique (see page 26).

13. Quilt around the rose-wreath shapes using tiny running stitches as described on page 28. Then quilt the lattice pattern, working from the centre of the rose-wreath outwards. Quilt all the border panels.

14. To assemble the quilt panels, join the centre panels in pairs, then join the pairs together to complete the central section, checking that all the quilting lanes join up to form continuous cross-hatching.

15. Join the bottom border and then the side borders to the central section, making mitred corners (see page 60).

16. Attach the final edge strip to the top of the quilt, right sides together.

17. Cut a length of polyester wadding measuring 250 x 5 cm (98½ x 2 in). Place the wadding inside the edge strip and roll the fabric strip over to the back to form a rolled edge. Tack in place.

18. Continue making a rolled edge all round the quilt by folding the right side over to the back, creating a rounded border about 5 cm (2 in) deep (see page 61). Curve the bottom corners slightly.

19. Hand hem the rolled edge with invisible hemming stitches.

ABOVE
Quilt artist: **Lesley Turpin-Delport**
Detail of the four-rose design used on the corners of each block.

ABOVE RIGHT
Quilt artist: **Lesley Turpin-Delport**
Detail of one of the rose-wreath panels. Notice the trapunto quilting on the roses and leaves, and the cross-hatch quilting on the background.

CENTRE, FAR RIGHT
Quilt artist: **Janet Roche**
An exquisite panel from Janet's quilt showing the fine two-strand embroidery details, trapunto and echo quilting.

CENTRE, RIGHT
Quilt artist: **Paulette Hodes**
Detail of a beautiful panel, showing trapunto quilting, candlewicking and embroidery. Note the colonial knots in the background.

RIGHT
Quilt artist: **Paulette Hodes**
Detail of a trapunto-quilted panel with a candlewick-quilted background. Note the use of French knots, extended French knots, stem stitch and raised chain stitch.

QUILTING DESIGN

STAINED-GLASS WINDOW DESIGN (Page 76)

APPLIQUÉ BOUQUET QUILT
(Page 88)

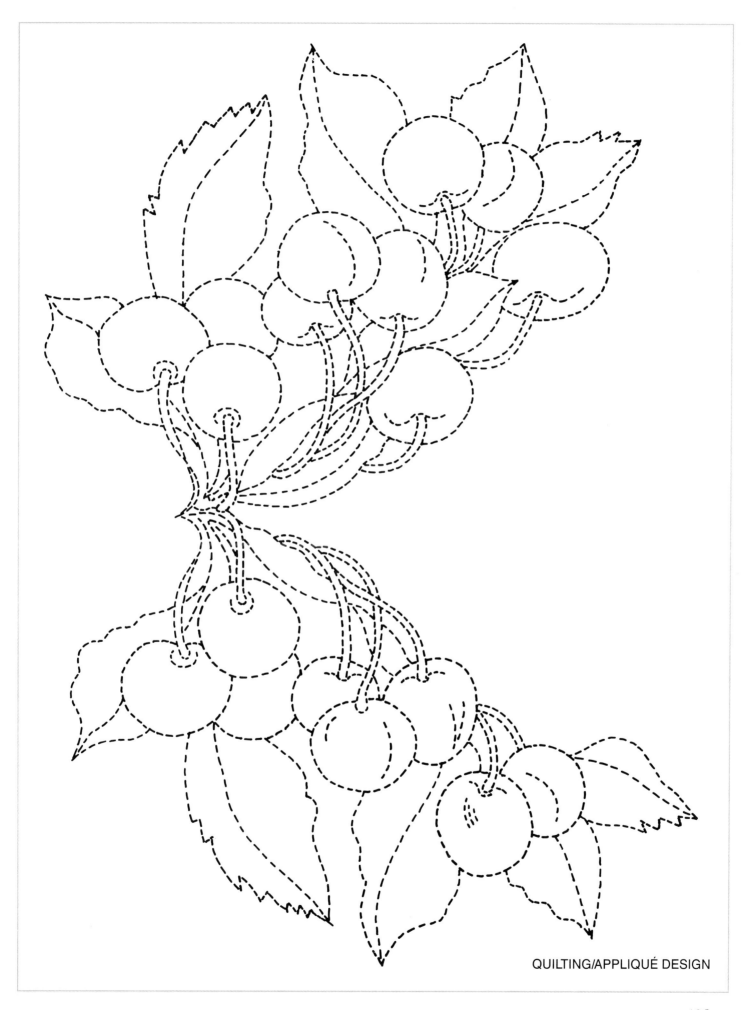

QUILTING/APPLIQUÉ DESIGN

BALTIMORE-STYLE APPLIQUÉ DESIGN

QUILTING/EMBROIDERY DESIGNS

112

QUILTING/EMBROIDERY DESIGNS

QUILTING/APPLIQUÉ DESIGN

QUILTING/EMBROIDERY DESIGN

QUILTING/EMBROIDERY DESIGN

QUILTING/EMBROIDERY DESIGN

QUILTING/EMBROIDERY DESIGN

QUILTING/EMBROIDERY DESIGN

QUILTING/EMBROIDERY DESIGN

QUILTING/EMBROIDERY DESIGN

ROSE-WREATH QUILT (Page 104)

ROSE-WREATH QUILT LAYOUT

QUILTING/EMBROIDERY DESIGN

QUILTING/EMBROIDERY DESIGN

BORDER QUILTING DESIGN

BORDER QUILTING DESIGN

CABLE QUILTING DESIGN

CABLE QUILTING DESIGN

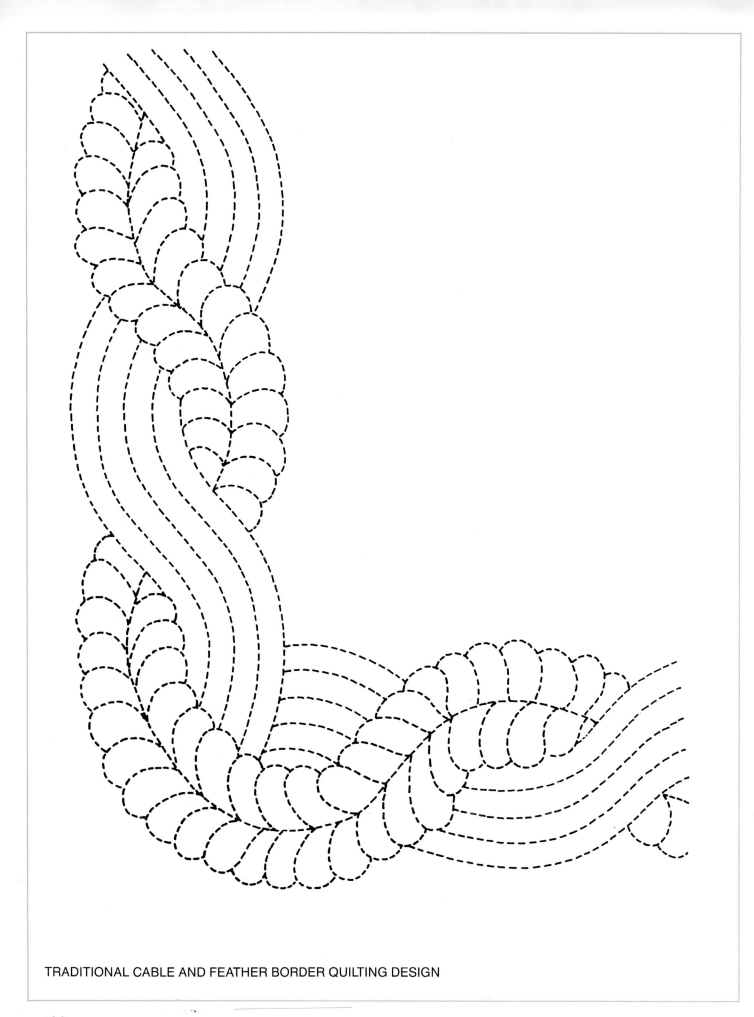

TRADITIONAL CABLE AND FEATHER BORDER QUILTING DESIGN

TRADITIONAL CURVED FEATHER WREATH   PART 1

QUILTING DESIGNS

QUILTING DESIGNS

QUILTING DESIGN

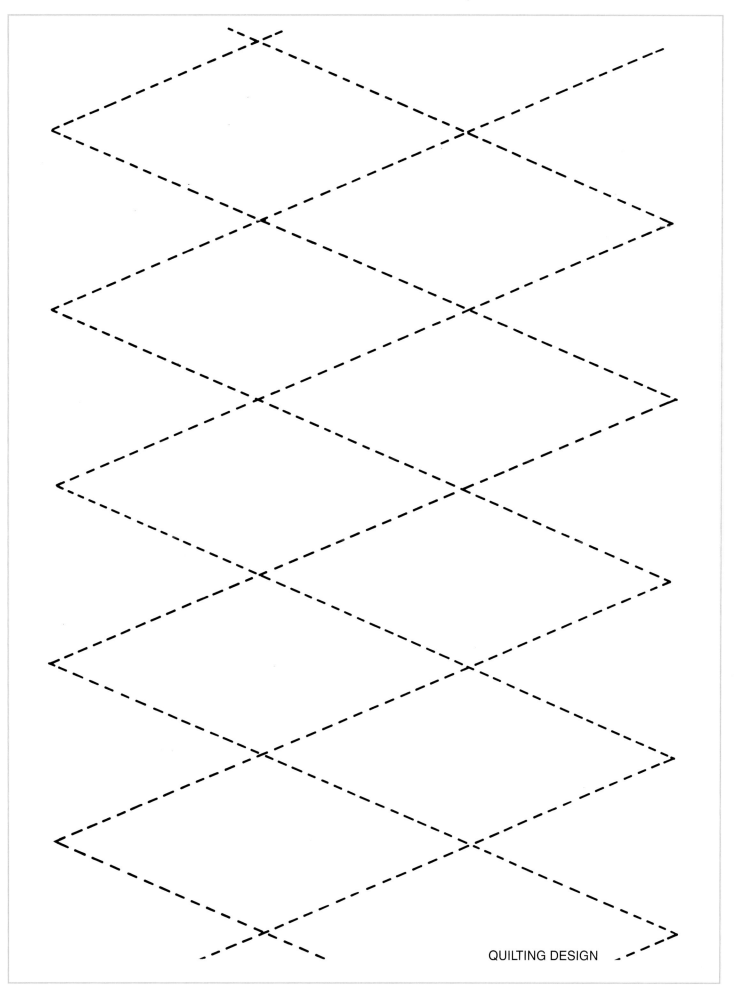
QUILTING DESIGN

QUILTING DESIGN

QUILTING DESIGNS

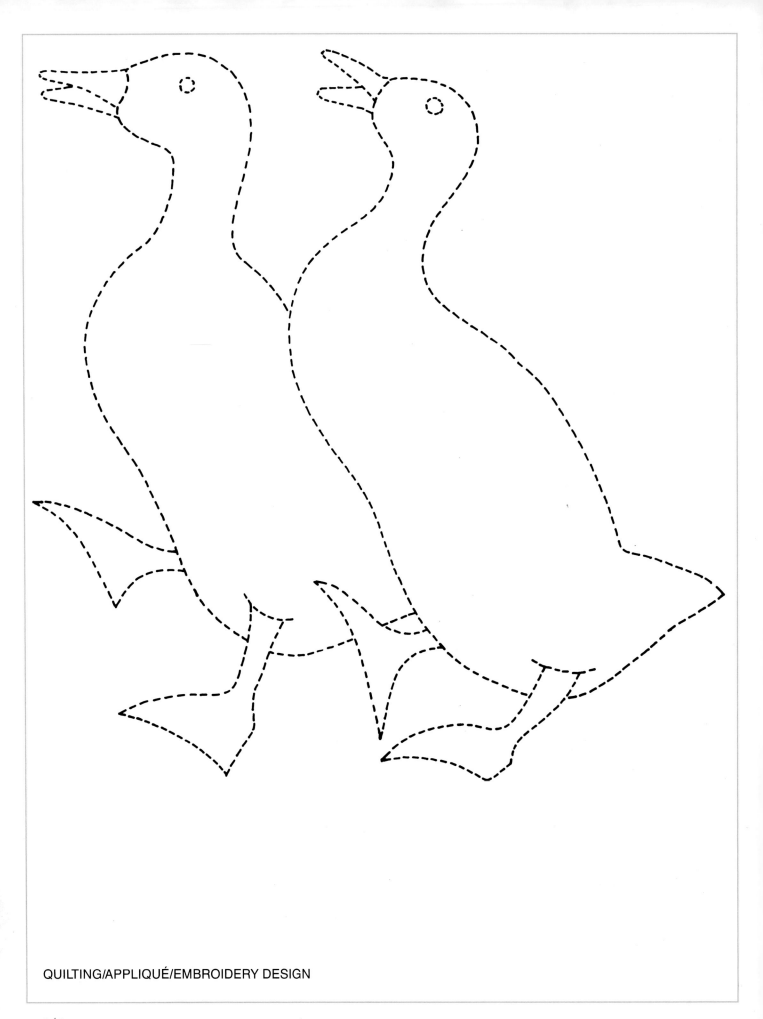

QUILTING/APPLIQUÉ/EMBROIDERY DESIGN

EMBROIDERY DESIGN

QUILTING/EMBROIDERY DESIGN

MINIATURE WHOLE-CLOTH QUILT DESIGN *DAISY GARLAND*

DESIGN INSPIRED BY THE AUTHOR'S KITCHEN TILES

QUILTING/EMBROIDERY DESIGN

MINIATURE WHOLE-CLOTH QUILT DESIGN *WATERLILIES*

MINIATURE WHOLE-CLOTH QUILT DESIGN *TRADITIONAL*

MINIATURE WHOLE-CLOTH QUILT DESIGN *HEDGEHOGS*

MINIATURE WHOLE-CLOTH QUILT DESIGN *FEATHERED HEART*

QUILTING/APPLIQUÉ DESIGN

QUILTING/APPLIQUÉ DESIGN

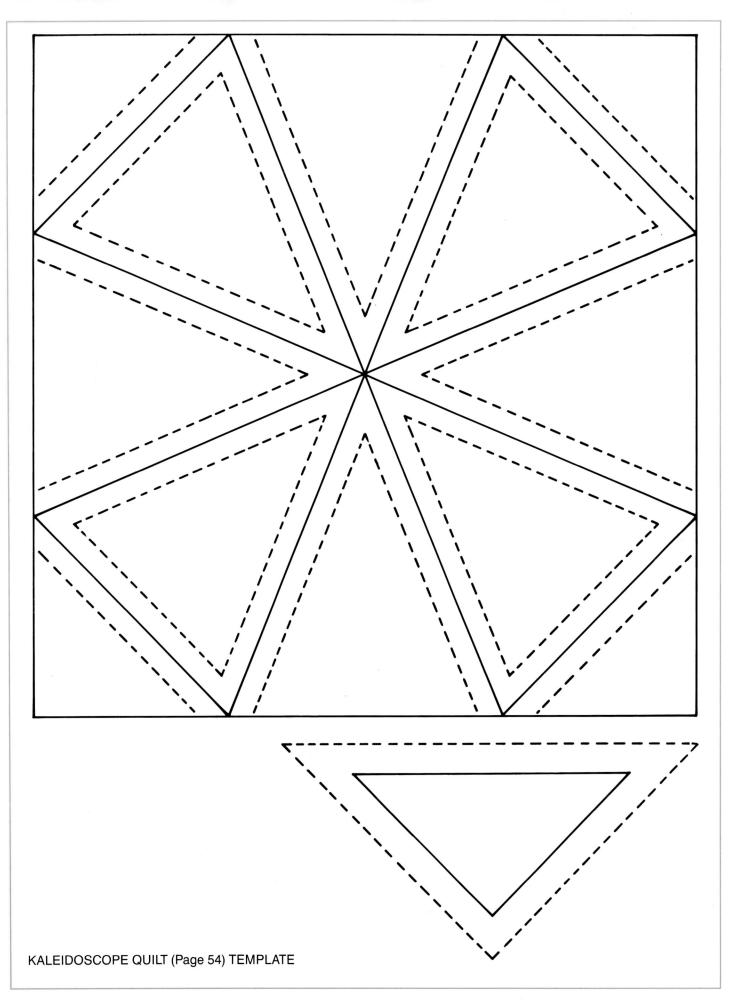

KALEIDOSCOPE QUILT (Page 54) TEMPLATE

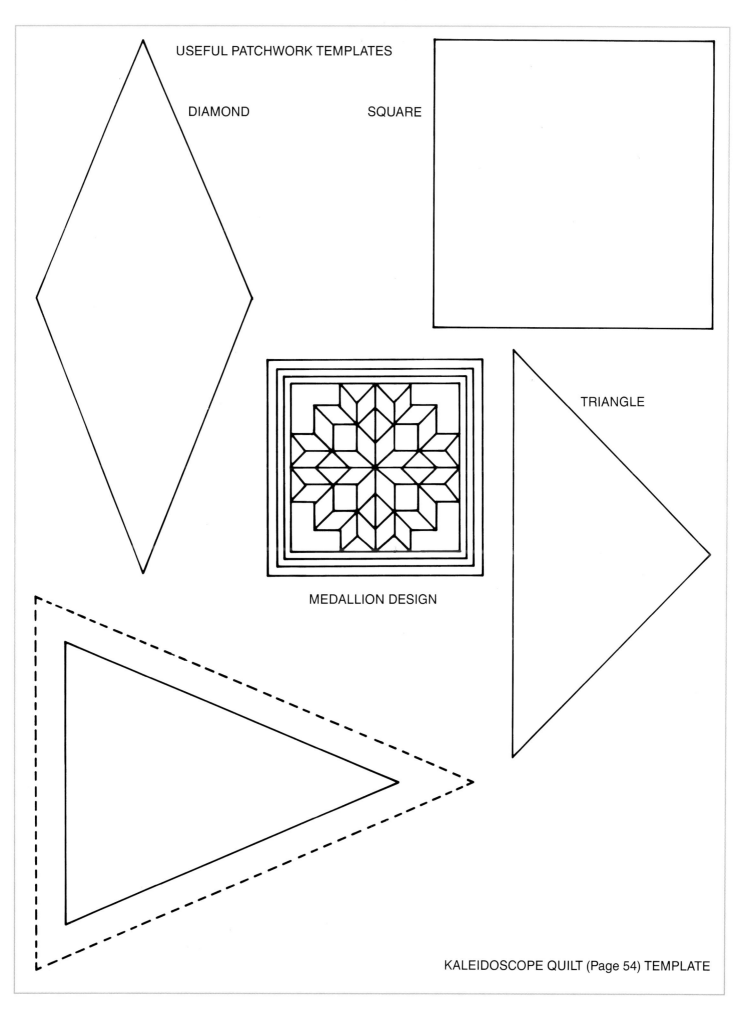

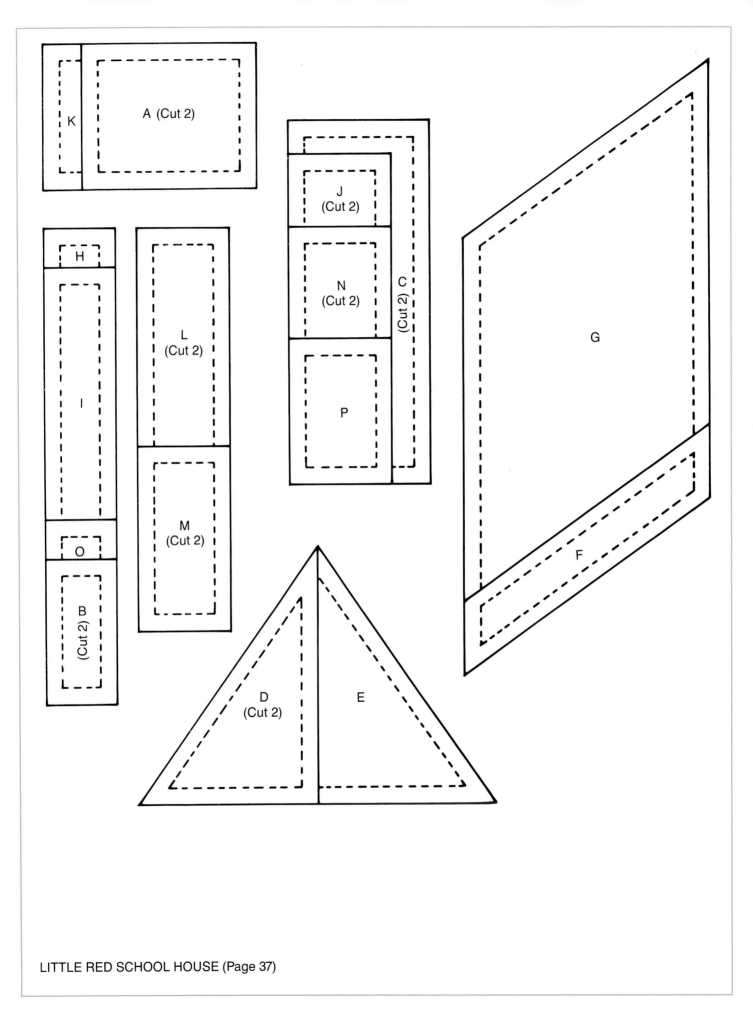

LITTLE RED SCHOOL HOUSE (Page 37)

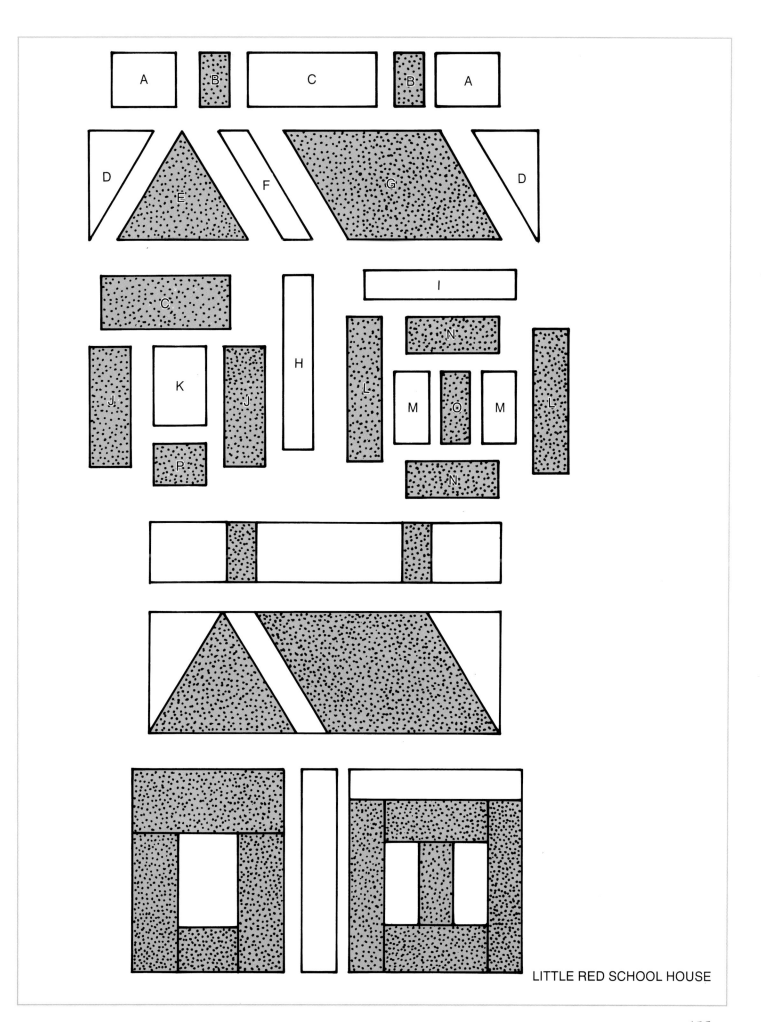

LITTLE RED SCHOOL HOUSE

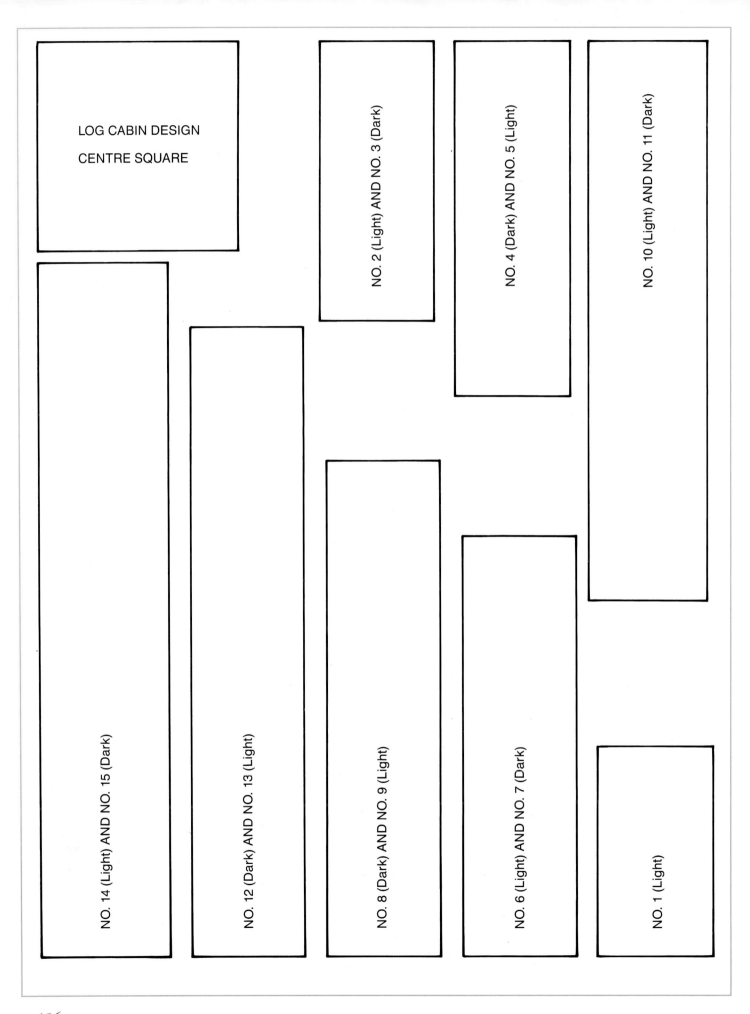

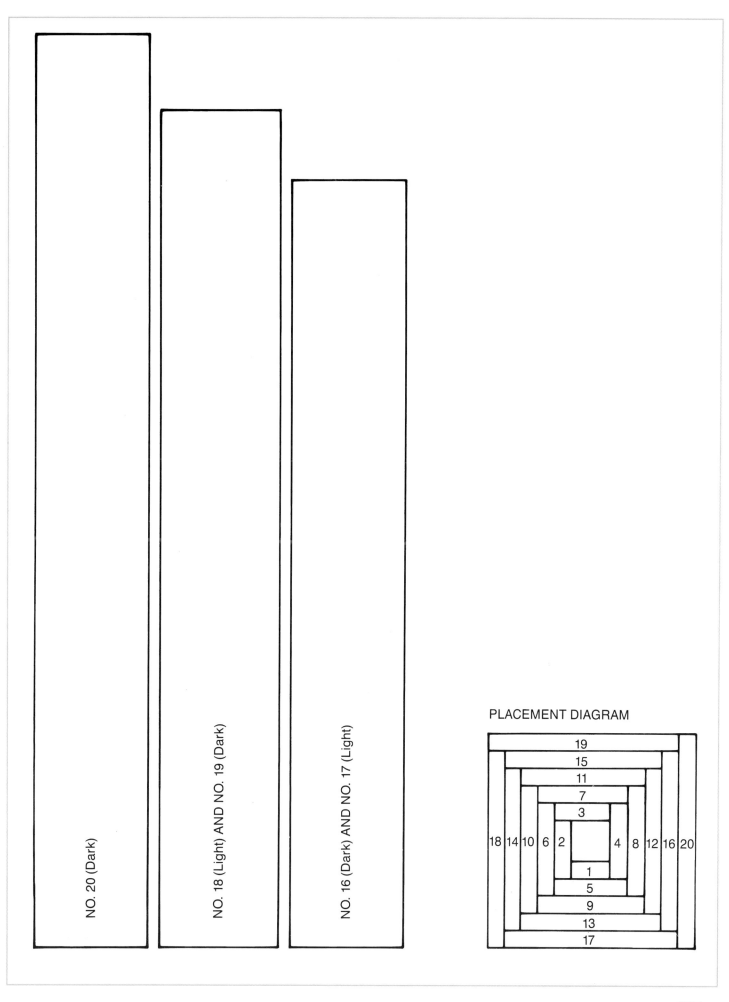

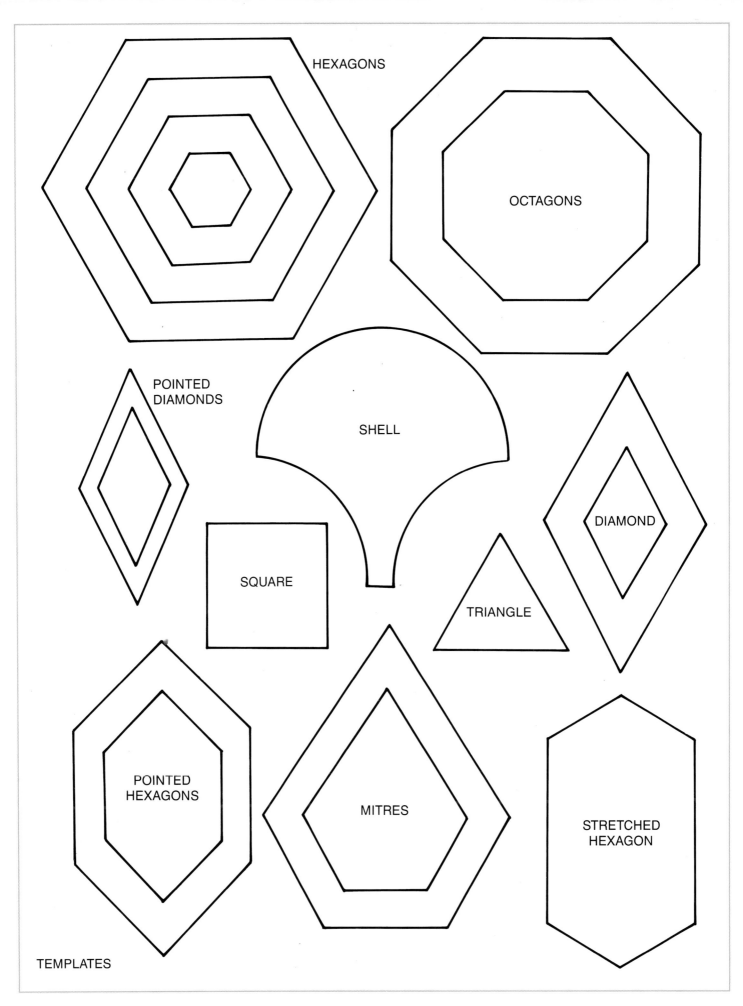

FURTHER READING

American Quilts and How to Make them by Carter Houck and Myron Miller (Pelham Books)
The Art of the Needle by Jan Beaney (Century Hutchinson)
Baltimore Beauties and Beyond by Elly Sienkiewicz (C+T Publishing)
Colour and Cloth, the Quiltmaker's Ultimate Workbook by Mary Coyne Penders (The Quilt Digest Press)
The Complete Book of Appliqué and Patchwork by Lesley Turpin-Delport (Struik Publishers)
The Complete Book of Quilting by Michele Walker (Francis Lincoln-Windward)
Crazy Quilts by Penny McMorris (E P Dutton, New York)
Crazy Quilt Stitches by Dorothy Bond (Eugene Print, Oregon)
Creative Appliqué to make and wear by Lesley Turpin-Delport (Struik Publishers)
Cut it Away by Marie Peacey
The Embroiderer's Garden by Thomasina Beck (David and Charles)
Erica Wilson's Embroidery Book by Erica Wilson (Faber and Faber, London)
Glorious Garments by Marie Peacey
The Great American Log Cabin Quilt Book by Carol Anne Wein (E P Dutton, New York)
Mola – Appliqué with a Difference by Marie Peacey
The Needlework Garden by Jane Iles (Century)
Painting on Cloth by Marie Peacey
The Pieced Quilt by Jonathan Holstein (New York Graphic Society, Boston)
The Poster Book of Quilts by Thos K Woodward and Blanche Greenstein (E P Dutton, New York)
Protea Designs – For Piecing and Quilting by Maretha Fourie
Quick Quilting, Make a Quilt this Weekend by Barbara Johannah (Drake Publishing Inc, New York and London)
The Quilt Digest by Kiracofe and Kile (San Francisco)
The Quilter's Album of Blocks and Borders by Jinny Beyer (E P M Publications Inc)
Quilting, Patchwork, Appliqué and Trapunto by Thelma R. Newman (George Allen and Unwin Ltd)
The Quiltmakers Handbook by Michael James (Prentice-Hall)
Scraps can be Beautiful by Jan Halgrimson
The South African Book of Patchwork and Appliqué by Lesley Turpin-Delport (Struik Publishers)

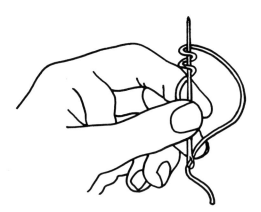

QUILTING TEACHERS

(Who have made a special contribution to this book)
Lesley Campbell and Julia Clephane, Knysna Loerie Quilters Guild. Tel: (0441) 90821.
Celia de Villiers, 43 Glouchester Road, Kensington 2094. Tel: (011) 616-6907.
Suzette Ehlers, 39 Baddrif Street, Sasolburg 9570. Tel: (016) 763-924.
Maretha Fourie, 19 George Street, Randburg 2194. Tel: (011) 787-9954.
Sandi Lotter, 24 Glenny Crescent, Lonehill, Johannesburg. Tel: (011) 465-1156.
Pat Parker and Jenny Williamson, 83 Westwold Way, Saxonwold, Johannesburg. Tel: (011) 726-8418 or (011) 646-8884.
Marie Peacey, P.O. Box 51, Parow 7500.
Margee Gough and Janet Roche, Lavender Blue, The Cobbles, 4th Avenue, Parkhurst, Johannesburg.
Jessica van Niekerk. Tel: (011) 678-9850.
Jolena van Rooyen, 1 Goedhart Crescent, Waverley, Bloemfontein. Tel: (051) 314-032.

For enquiries about Quilt Teachers, contact the South African Quilt Teachers Association, 5 Protea Close, Pinelands 7405.

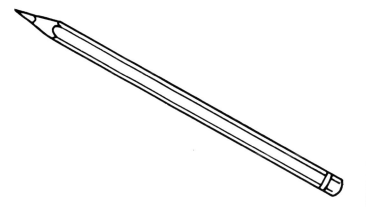

QUILTERS SHOPPING GUIDE

TRANSVAAL
Baih's Materials, Grootfontein Centre, Sasolburg.
Tel: (016) 762-2328
Country Patchwork, Ruimsig, 383 Stallion Road, Roodepoort.
Tel: (011) 958-1900.
Lavender Blue, The Cobbles, 4th Avenue, Parkhurst, Johannesburg.
Les Designs, 21 Orchards Road, Orchards, Johannesburg (Kits, books and franchise teacher network). Tel: (011) 728-3408.
Stitch Talk, Verwoerdburgstad. Tel: (012) 663-2035.

NATAL
Kalicoscope, P O Box 4206, Durban 4000. Tel: (031) 29-2082.
Quilters Companion, Margaret le Roux, P O Box 1447, Wandsbeck 3631. (Quilting rulers and squares). Tel: (031) 864-163.

CAPE PROVINCE
Pickles and Patchwork, Pinelands, Cape Town.
Tel: (021) 531-0617
Pied Piper, Port Elizabeth. Tel: (041) 52-3090.
The Craft Gallery, P O Box 2062, Beacon Bay, East London.
Tel: (0431) 47-2420.

INDEX

Bold numbers indicate photographs

Added binding (French binding) 60
Afro-American quilts 58-59
Amish 12, 48
Ankerman, Annamarie **47**
Appliqué
  Baltimore 69
  bouquet quilt 88
  direct 84
  double fabric 84
  double vilene 84
  fabric collage 80
  free-style 80
  hand 69
  in-laid 70
  machine 84
  on-laid methods 69
  planning the design 68
  quilting machine 84
  reverse 78
  selecting the fabrics 68
  shadow 74
  stained-glass 74, 76
  stitches 69, 70
  stitching corners 70
  stitching curves 70
  to make circles 70
  transferring the design 68

Back stitch 28, 92
Baltimore appliqué 69
Baltimore quilts 72
Batting *see* Wadding 10
Berkowitz, Marion **90-91**
Bias binding
  flowers 71
  how to make 74
  stems 70
Boltar, Marion **73**
Borders
  corners of 60
  how to assemble 60
  how to choose 17
  prairie point 63
Botha, Mariette **63**
Buds, in-laid 70
Bullion
  knot 93
  looped 96
  rosebud 93
Button quilting 103
Buttonhole stitch 72, 92
  semi-detached 95

Campbell, Lesley **73**
Candlewick embroidery 102
Chain stitch 92
  detached 92
  raised 93
  whipped 95
Clephane, Julia **19**, **36**
Coertzen, Marietjie **72**
Colonial knot 28, 102
Colour wheel 12
Competitions, quilt 22
Continuous curve quilting 31
Corded quilting 27
Couching 92
Crooke, Jackie **2**, **3**
Cross-hatch quilting 84, 104

Delport, Hennie **78**
Delport, Nicola **23**
Design, creating your own 18
De Villiers, Celia **18**, **80-83**
Diagonal quilting 28
Double fabric technique 84
Double vilene technique 84
Druian, Rachelle **88-89**

Echo quilting 26, 31, 84
Ehlers, Suzette **27**, **57**

Embroidery
  candlewick 102
  hand 92
  requirements 92
  stitches 92, 93, 94, 95, 96
  to transfer the design 92
Enlarging the design 68

Fabric collage 80
Fabric
  for appliqué 68
  for piecing 34
  for quilting 10
  to colour your own 15
Faulds, Jutta **21**
Feather stitch 96
Filler quilting 26
Flat-fell seam 88
Fletcher, Jackie **15**
Fly stitch 93
  extended 93
Fourie, Maretha **56-57**
Fouché, Lydia **13**
Foulner, Ann **100**
Frames, quilting 11
Free-motion quilting 31
Free-style appliqué 80
French binding *see* Added binding
French knot 92
  extended 92
Funston, Sue **15**

Gilks, Jeanette **59**
Gough, Margee **17**, **37**, **38**, **38**, **49**, **51**, **53**
Grant, Claire **72**, **96**, **99**
Grid quilting 31
Grub rose 93

Hackman, Lee **24-25**
Hand appliqué 68
Hand embroidery 92
Hand quilting 28
Hearder, Valerie **20**
Hidden wells 50
Hodes, Paulette **105**
Hoops, quilting 11

In-laid appliqué, buds 70

Kaleidoscope quilt 54
Kaplan, Glenda **85**
Katz, Edelgard **87**
Klaasen, Gerda **47**
Kruger, June **56**

Laid work 93
Lattice quilting 28
Lazy daisy filling stitch 96
Loerie Quilters Guild **77**
Le Roux, Margaret **5**, **23**, **62**
Lewis, Lesley **27**
Log cabin (fold over) patchwork 40
  pineapple 52
Lombard, Lina **22**
Lotter, Sandi **30**, **31**

Machine appliqué 84
Machine quilting 31
Marking tools 10
Mattress measurements 17
McDonald, Joey **57**
Mola *see* Reverse appliqué 78
Morris, Mary **27**
Muter, Ettie **43**

Needles, for quilting 10
Nine-patch quilt 48
  Philip's radiant 64

On-laid hand appliqué 69
Outline quilting 26

Paper backing 34
Paper piecing method 52, 54
Pattern and colour 12, 13
Peacey, Marie **78**, **79**

Pearce, Denise **99**
Pekinese stitch 93
Perry, Pat **35**
Philip's radiant nine-patch quilt 64
Piecing
  Afro-American quilts 58
  attaching borders 60
  basic nine-patch 48
  by hand 35
  by machine 40
  Hidden wells 50
  Kaleidoscope 54
  log cabin 40
  Philip's radiant nine-patch quilt 64
  pineapple log cabin 52
  preparing the patches 34
  single-seam method 35
  strip piecing 46
  templates 34
  to finish the quilt 60
Piecing and quilting 33-65
Pineapple log cabin 52
Planning the appliqué design 68
Portuguese border stitch 94
Prairie points 63

Quilt
  appliqué bouquet 88
  competitions 22
  layouts 16
  Philip's radiant nine-patch 64
  to assemble 103
  trapunto candlewick 104
Quilt-as-you-go 103
Quilting
  Baltimore quilts 72
  button 103
  by hand 28
  by machine 31
  continuous curve 31
  corded 27
  cross-hatching 72
  designs (stencils) 31
  diagonal 28
  echo 26, 31, 72, 84
  filler 26
  frames 11
  free-motion 31
  hoops 11
  grid 31
  in the ditch 26
  lattice 28
  needles 10
  outline 26
  preparation 26
  quilting in patterns 26
  rocker 28
  rulers 10
  stencils 10
  thread 10, 31
  tied 103
  tools for marking 10
  trapunto 26
  twin needling 84
Quilting stitches 28

Reverse appliqué 78
Roche, Janet **22**, **27**, **71**, **98**, **102**, **105**
Rocker quilting 28
Rosebuds, three-dimensional 71
Roumanian stitch 93
Ryder, Moira **101**

Sarang, Sabera **45**
Sashing 16
  joining block with 103
Satin stitch 93
  long and short 93
Schlesinger, Denise **6**, **87**
Scott, Isabel **4**, **39**
Scott, Sally **58**
Segal, Leonie **14**
Self binding 61
Sessel, Blanche **98**
Shadow appliqué 74
Single stitching 28
Single-seam method (American) 35
Sittig, Susan **45**

Sleeve, to make 22
Snowflake block 69
Spider's web 93
Split stitch 93
Stab stitch 28
Stained-glass appliqué 74, 76
  to quilt 76
Starke, Roy **4**, **32-33**
Stem stitch 92
  raised 94
Stitches
  appliqué 69, 70
  back 92
  bullion knot 93
  bullion rosebud 93
  buttonhole 72, 92
  chain 92
  colonial knot 102
  couching 92
  detached chain 92
  extended fly 93
  extended French knot 92
  feather 96
  fly 93
  French knot 92
  grub rose 93
  laid work 93
  lazy daisy filling 96
  lazy daisy 92
  long and short satin 93
  looped bullion knot 96
  Pekinese 93
  Portuguese border 94
  raised chain 93
  raised stem 94
  Roumanian 93
  satin 93
  semi-detached buttonhole 95
  spider's web 93
  split 93
  stem 92
  striped woven band 94
  thorn 96
  turkey work 95
  weaving 93
  wheat ear 96
  whipped chain stitch 95
Stitching in the ditch 31
Storm, Annamarie **75**
Strip piecing 46
  basic nine-patch quilt 48
  Hidden wells 50
Striped woven band 94

Taute, Annetjie **45**
Templates/patterns 34, 105-158
Textile sandwich 26
Thimbles 10
Thorn stitch 96
Thread 10, 31
Tied quilting 103
Tools for marking 10
Transferring the design 68
Trapunto
  candlewick quilt 104
  quilting 26
Turkey work 95
Turpin-Delport, Lesley **11**, **29**, **48**, **65**, **74**, **98**, **104**, **105**
Twin needling 84

Van Aiden, Riet **17**
Van der Riet, Anne **44**
Van Niekerk, Jessica **1**, **38**
Van Rensburg, Nanna **29**
Van Rensburg, Salli **96**
Van Rooyen, Jolena **66-67**, **41**, **42**, **55**
Village quilters, Kloof **8-9**

Wadding 10
  for machine quilting 31
  to join 10
Weaving stitch 93
Wheat ear stitch 96
Whole-cloth quilts 29
Wulfsohn, Madge **94**, **95**, **100**

Yates, Adrienne **37**, **42**, **85**, **87**, **101**